PARADISE

REGAINED

To C.L. Sulzberger with friendship —
this foto from prison
1936. because in prison
of Yugoslavia of which
I was one of the crea-
tors photography is
forbidden.

23. 8. 1977.

Milovan Djilas

PARADISE
REGAINED

Memoir of a Rebel

C. L. Sulzberger

PRAEGER

New York
Westport, Connecticut
London

Library of Congress Cataloging-in-Publication Data

Sulzberger, C. L. (Cyrus Leo), 1912–
    Paradise regained : memoir of a rebel / C. L. Sulzberger.
        p.   cm.
    Bibliography: p.
    Includes index.
    ISBN 0-275-93076-9 (alk. paper).   ISBN 0-275-93077-7 (pbk. : alk.
paper)
    1. Djilas, Milovan, 1911–   2. Dissenters—Yugoslavia—
Biography. 3. Authors, Serbian—20th century—Biography.
I. Title.
DR1305.D56S85 1989
949.7'023'0924—dc19   88-9719

Library of Congress Catalog Card Number: 88-9719
ISBN: 0-275-93076-9
      0-275-93077-7 (pbk)
First published in 1989

Praeger Publishers, One Madison Avenue, New York, NY 10010
A division of Greenwood Press, Inc.

Printed in the United States of America

The paper used in this book complies with the
Permanent Paper Standard issued by the National
Information Standards Organization (Z39.48-1984).

10 9 8 7 6 5 4 3 2 1

This book is for Eda, who nursed its inception—from the banks of the Tara to the banks of the Sava and finally to the Danube and, in the end, to the Seine—wisely, sympathetically, and with skill.

Contents

PARADISE
REGAINED

1

Paradise Lost

In 1986, after twenty-nine years without liberty, or with restricted liberty, Milovan Djilas, Yugoslavia's most famous dissident and long-term political prisoner, became a free man. Djilas' greatest enterprise during his imprisonment was the translation into Serbo-Croatian, his native language, of John Milton's *Paradise Lost,* a translation that was, until very recently, still under ban in his native country because for some strange reason his books had not yet been released to the public, regardless of subject matter. But after twelve years in prison—both under the prewar royal regime and the postwar communist regime, and including thirty months of solitary confinement—and after a final seventeen years of liberty to travel only inside Yugoslavia, but with no permission to leave (excepting one instance), he is now free to come and go anywhere he wishes.

Djilas says he chose to translate Milton's great work because Paradise clearly symbolizes "freedom." Now, he says happily, after returning from a celebratory London visit:

I feel the freest man in Yugoslavia. Maybe I'm not but that's how I feel. I feel freer than Tito. He depended on support for his power. For me this is not important, because I am truly free; nobody can take anything important from me. I'm only not free in relation to Stefanie, my wife, and my son, Aleksa. But I love them.

I have learned that it is possible to regain Paradise only if it has been lost. The "loss" is simply "idealized." The Paradise "regained" in my case is real. Without suffering, Paradise cannot be regained. I am only the slave of my wife and son. They suffered more than I did. I'm a free man, an absolutely free man, because they didn't ever touch me in the heart. I feel freer than you who are a free man from a free country.

Djilas, who is seventy-six, has had an arduous life—as underground conspirator, as Partisan soldier (with the rank of Colonel General), and as tough and active ideologue. He started to translate *Paradise Lost* in prison, during 1964, when he was under sentence for opposition to Tito's regime. He chose Milton's poem as his subject because the English poet had disclosed strong political convictions in his symbolism, and because of the poet's endorsement of "patience and heroic martyrdom." Also, Djilas thought the poem's absence from Yugoslav literature was a notable lacuna.

It was not a logical selection in many ways. Djilas' English was far from perfect; writing materials in prison were few. However, he labored for more than two years, with dictionaries provided by friends, and actually wrote out large parts of the text on toilet paper with rudimentary pen and ink, the only tools available. Later he benefited from the critical help of a well-disposed professor of English literature.

When he emerged from prison, he found that not even Milton could be published in Yugoslavia, if Djilas were the translator. An American publisher of Yugoslav extraction has printed numerous copies of the Serbo-Croatian *Paradise*, but it has yet to be issued in Yugoslavia. Although he is free now, Djilas is not considered "morally" rehabilitated.

Milton's Satan, first among the archangels, was flung out of heaven for manifesting the hubris of aspiring to divinity. He is depicted as a wicked tempter of humanity, like the serpent in the Garden of Eden. To spread sin among men in the form of a serpent was Satan's method of revenge against God.

It is a shame for the average Yugoslav that Djilas' work is not available, even though Milton's original English iambic meter had to be reworked into Serbian types of Alexandrine meter. Djilas recalls:

Being in prison I thought about Milton; he was also a revolutionary at the end, disillusioned and literally mad. And I thought that our language had no such important work and I was ambitious to be the first to translate this into the Serbian language.

Milton, blind, defended Cromwell's regicides, was harassed by Restoration authorities, and changed his religion from Catholicism to Anglicanism and then to Presbyterianism. Djilas shifted from orthodox Marxism to Stalinism to Titoism to anti-Titoist Marxism and in the end to democracy and negation of "isms".

Despite his many accomplishments in Yugoslavia as a revolutionist, soldier, politician, diplomat, and author, the existing post-Tito regime until 1988 seemed eager to keep his name forgotten—the only reason for refusing to let him write for publication at home. His works can be and are printed abroad. Djilas used to say wryly, "I am permitted to travel anywhere but only to publish abroad." This has started to change in 1988.

Among his hard-earned insights into religion and freedom:

I think pessimism is futile and I think optimism is naive, considering the human condition. What I have learned and suffered is categorical; a man without faith, without ideas and ideals, can be imagined only as a man in a world of absolute void . . . the world of his nonexistence. Although I am not a religious man I think religion will exist as long as men exist. . . .

★★★

One thing is certain: I am not a Marxist. I am not a religious man but I know that a human being must have conscience and morality. I agree with what religion teaches: that man must believe in something. But not in God.

★★★

Now I have regained my Paradise, of freedom. Freedom to live freely, walk freely, see whom I wish, go where I want, anywhere in the world; to be with my wife wherever we are and to go together to see my son, now in England where we have just visited, perhaps soon in America, at Harvard, where he has been awarded a fellowship.

★★★

Maybe this is not complete freedom. I don't believe complete freedom, absolute freedom, is possible. Equality is not possible in human society. But revolutions have come about because of the belief in equality and absolute freedom.

★★★

I am satisfied that I am a free man. That is the meaning of Paradise.

Djilas is now near the end of his life and enjoys indifferent health. Nevertheless, this conviction of inner freedom radiates from his smiling face and active figure. Although he had been hospitalized only recently before receiving his passport to travel, he still personifies vigor. The perceptible return of an old man's self-confidence in freedom's "paradise" is a heartening sight.

2

Fisherman

Milovan Djilas has a passion for fishing, above all for trout, a sport he learned as a boy in Montenegro. His modest home was situated on a bluff above the fast-flowing Tara River. Where the path leading down to the narrow road into Podbišće (his native village) joined the Tara there were (and still are) two splendid pools between the tumbling rapids.

His teacher was an old peasant who fished each eddy with patient care, using a line made out of skeins of hair plucked from a horse's tail and hooks that he made from his wife's discarded steel knitting needles. Milovan recalls:

It wasn't possible to ascertain whether he fished so much because he enjoyed doing so or because his family needed the extra food. He didn't show any enthusiasm when he had success or despair when he caught nothing.

As a result of this experience I made a rod for myself of hazelnut wood. But the tip was of even harder wood. I made a line of braided white horsehair from a horse's tail. It was very difficult to find the properly long and properly white tail of a horse and pluck hairs until you had enough to braid them together. The leader I used was gut and imported. I bought it and the hooks. I put worms and insects on the hooks. One of my favorites was a kind of green-banded locust.[1]

It is not surprising that Djilas, a thoughtful, contemplative, scholarly, and philosophical man who was brought up close to nature in a region of mountains carved apart by streams should be an ardent fisherman. He is psychologically and temperamentally attracted to the ancient sport. In this respect he resembles Isaak Walton, the "Compleat Angler," who was not gifted enough to use a fly, although such a lure had been known for centuries, but who wrote brilliantly and reflected deeply, stimulated by a strange companionship with his piscine friends, attracted to his hook by worms.

Nowadays, almost every spring or summer I manage to take off time to angle with Milovan in Yugoslavia, from Slovenia and Eastern Serbia in the north to Herzegovina and Montenegro in the deep south where he was reared. Fishermen can talk without inhibition to each other, touching on hidden, secret thoughts. Djilas once confided to me, sitting beside the gurgling Mlava River:

I think people like fishing because there is some eternal connection between man and fish, especially trout. Trout is the highest form of fish for man to associate with. . . .

I think if I didn't fish with such enthusiasm I would not have rebelled against the Central Committee of the Communist Party. My thoughts became clarified as I fished. My individuality and integrity developed. Subconsciously I changed. . . . [2]

Fishing for sport is one of the oldest amusements of man and also perhaps the most contemplative. It is said that just over two thousand years ago the first trout fly was tied by a Macedonian named Ichthyoulkos, one of the earliest Balkan fishermen. During the first and second centuries A.D. it is known that angling was practiced in many parts of the Roman Empire, presumably including Montenegro, before the earliest Slavs arrived.

It is, of course, the delight of a trout fisherman to find the haunts of his underwater friend (always, for some marvelous reason, set in a place of beauty); to approach silently, carefully, to hook him fatefully with wiliness—and then to release him, bestowing mankind's greatest gift, freedom. I myself have released more than ninety percent of those I ever brought to net or shore.

Fishing—any kind of fishing—is of immense value as a tranquilizer to people swept up in life's complicated hurly burly. I can provide confirmation of this in the instance of Milovan, who acknowledges that angling probably helped to alter his philosophy of life.

Djilas is completely Montenegrin. Beside a stream, he consistently demonstrates his people's vitality and cleverness in his enticement of the wily trout. When unable to leave his country—as so many thousands do—he depended more than ever on the consolation of fishing.

For a long time, when Djilas was not in prison, I had become accustomed to calling on him during my visits to Yugoslavia. It was during these discussions, in his Belgrade study or in the sitting room—dominated by a painting of the late Lazar Vozarević, a work that is dark, menacing, part Byzantine and part Aztec in appearance—that we first began to talk of shooting and fishing. He could not obtain a passport to come to my house in Greece and shoot birds. And in any case, he admitted to great eagerness for a trout-fishing expedition—if he could ever regain membership in the Fishermen's Association and obtain a license. (It would have been obvious folly for a man under police supervision to risk fishing illegally.)

On May 2, 1979, I stopped off in Belgrade with my dog Christopher Beagle and the two of us were as usual promptly invited to dinner. Milovan's eyes gleamed as we discussed various areas of the country said to be rich in trout. He promised at last to make a direct application for renewed membership in the angling organization. To my delight, a few weeks later he sent me a letter saying he had regained the status of a legal angler.

On my return he was like a small boy on holiday. Stefica, his wife, told me he had purchased a new spinning rod and reel as well as various little spoons and other artificial lures. (Few Yugoslavs go in for fly fishing. At the stream we eventually worked for trout. I was not only the sole foreigner but also the sole angler who confined his efforts to dry flies, frail leaders, and a light bamboo rod.)

The village Djilas selected as our base was Žagubica in that region of northeastern Serbia called the Homolje, bordering both Rumania and Bulgaria. He began his survey after he had decided to go personally to the headquarters of the anglers' association and apply for readmission.

The same man who had been secretary of the Belgrade organization a quarter of a century prior, when Djilas was expelled, still remained secretary. He was nervous when he recognized his visitor's well-known face. He said: "You know, I gave you your first membership. Then there were some political problems." That was all. He made out a new card and Milovan paid his dues.

We drove in my Volkswagen along back roads south of the Danube, Djido chatting happily and at length about one fish, known in English as the *huchen* (from German) and in most Slavic languages as the *hucho* (from the Latin, *Hucho hucho*), a large, elongated salmonoid that inhabits many river systems leading into the Danube.

When we came to Gornjak and the convent and church of Czar Lazar (who lost the famous Kosovo battle of 1389 but remains the Serbian hero) we visited the lovely chapel with its fourteenth century frescoes.

Gornjak was our introduction to the Homolje and to the lovely winding river Mlava whose upper waters we were to explore. The Homolje is a soft, rolling area replete with woods and streams. It has a mysterious history. When I first visited Yugoslavia in the 1930s there used to be a weird ancient dancing ceremony in one corner each spring.

Every peasant, including very old and very young, would gather at the mystic rite. To the tune of pipes and primitive stringed instruments everyone, even the infants, would join in a ceremonial dance. Then all females, from toddling babies to elderly crones, would succumb to a fainting trance. When the last lay unconscious, the men and boys would dance about them, chewing garlic. They then went to a nearby brook, filled their mouths with water, returned still dancing, and spat through crossed knives on the faces of the women and girls, who promptly regained consciousness. Even baby girls who couldn't yet speak were affected as much as their mothers and grandmothers.

There were two restaurants in the little village of Žagubica where we made our headquarters. For our midday meal we preferred a place grandiosely named the "Motel," a small hostelry on the bank of the deep pool where the Mlava springs suddenly out of the mountainside. Fishing was banned in the pool although large trout could be seen feeding.

In the evening we supped at the Homoljac, which means "man from the Homolje." Locally this place—which was simple, unpretentious, run by only three people, and excellent—was known as a *privat*, or privately-owned business. A family plus up to two employees may operate such an enterprise in Communist Yugoslavia.

We ate there nightly with a few other habitués, all fishermen. One, a pleasant retired criminal detective, aged 58, looked like a successful central European banker, well dressed, always puffing a good briar pipe. Since his son, who accompanied him, appeared a good deal older than his 23 years, they seemed like brothers. Both were successful with their spinners and showed us some splendid trout.

Another angler, Brača, sartorially elegant, used to come here with his agreeable West German wife. He told us he was staying at the "Motel" once, when he had been unable to catch anything in the Mlava's legal stretches. So one dark night he put a large hook, baited with meat, on a strong weighted line and flung it out of his window, which was just above the forbidden pool. In short order he had a strike from a large trout and hauled it up, flapping. "I couldn't catch anything, anywhere," he said with a smug smile, "so I started breaking the law."

This prompted me to recount the story of the seventeenth century lecher who was visiting France's famed Prince de Condé at his chateau of Chantilly, a beautiful structure girdled by a moat filled with enormous carp protected against fishermen. One night the lecher, who was also an avid angler, tossed a strong line, hooked and baited, out of his window and soon hauled up an immense five-foot fish.

As he freed it from the barb there was a pounding at the door. Rather than lose his prize, the guest flung back the cover of his bed and thrust the carp inside, hiding his tackle. An instant later Condé entered and, impolitely curious, observed much wriggling inside the bed. He flung off the spread, disclosing its slimy secret. "Even from you, my friend, I had not expected so strange an eccentricity," he observed.

Milovan, Brača, and his wife were delighted.

The Mlava was supervised by a very evil-looking, nervous, disagreeably mannered fish warden who rode around on a bicycle, inspecting licenses. He was short, thin, with sullen, lupine features and a sporty imitation Tyrolean hat. Milovan and I first met him when we were examining the neighborhood and had discovered a trout hatchery whose fingerlings were used to supply the whole network of Homolje streams.

The warden seemed courteous but more than his appearance was to his discredit. While Djilas was talking to him, I asked permission in my pidgin Serbo-Croatian to examine his tackle. He agreed. It was an ordinary cheap spinning rig with nylon line and a slight lead weight about fourteen inches above the hook. Around the hook was fastened a fat, slimy, live worm!

Apart from the fish-warden—and it is possible his appearance and uneasy manner plus the worm counted unfairly against him— everyone we met was exceptionally agreeable. Milovan was convinced the local police had been alerted to be on the look-out for him as a result of the well-known bugging of our conversations on his telephone. People in Žagubica, including the local chief of police, were unusually affable to both of us. I had the feeling that there was special respect as well as friendship for Milovan.

As for me—I expect I was the first American most of them had ever seen. The last foreigner anyone could recall in the neighborhood had been an attaché from London's embassy in Belgrade, who had come on a fishing trip about ten years earlier. A fly-fisherman, he was still known as "the mad Englishman."

The Homolje is unusually pleasant. Both the countryside and the human atmosphere are tranquil. The gentle stream—about five to eight yards wide and one to three deep—is hard on the fly-fisherman because—thank heavens—nothing is done to trim away the willows and bushes, to clean out the logs and tree-roots, or in any way to deprive the trout of such natural advantage as they may use. Since they are all brown trout (known as *fario* to most Europeans) and therefore shy, clever, and also very tasty, the job of depositing a dry fly a few inches in front of a feeding fish, landing it softly and avoiding all the trouble lurking behind on a false cast, requires meticulous attention.

And when (as is my custom) one wades the softly flowing waters in blue jeans and felt-soled shoes, not boots, one feels the caressive stream on the legs and one's mood becomes generous, tolerant, and open-spirited. Moreover, when as is so often the case, one has to scramble out of the river, and fight a way through tangled brambles and trees toward another and unknown pool, blocked by rapids or impassable depths, it is pleasant to walk through high-standing fields of corn and flowered meadows where shepherdesses tend their flocks while twisting wool into thread on hand spindles; or to watch the peasant women in gaily colored shawls and heavy skirts, tossing hay with primitive wooden pitchforks. Here and there, across one or another branch of the Mlava, extends a rickety wicker bridge or even a span comprising one bent, single tree-trunk beside which stands a nobbly, rudimentary handrail.

When we started our pursuit of the prey Djilas was nervous. He hadn't fished for a quarter of a century and wasn't sure how he would fare. At first he couldn't handle his spinners (which he calls "blinkers," German fashion) very adeptly. After a quarter of a century one tends to lose the rhythm in any sport. Also, he was pale and not entirely proof against fatigue. A wiry, compact man, he nevertheless possesses impressive reserves of strength.

The only noise apart from the gurgling of the rivulet was the sound of birds and an occasional rustle of leaves. Every now and then there would be an enormous flight of starlings over the still, motionless corn, through the mosquito-filled evening air. I was impressed by the atmosphere of utter peace. At one point, working upstream, I saw two turkeys and eight ducks lethargically lying in the shade beside the silently gliding water.

We fished three full days and enjoyed our share of fun after careful, hard work. Milovan had little luck with his new spinning rig. He caught one nice brown in a fine pool but when he left the pool to clean his conquest, he returned to find it had been taken over by two other "blinker" fishermen who put down the remaining inhabitants for the rest of the day with their splatter of hardware. But in the gentle, fragrant air amid rustling willow tendrils and corn tassels, this gave us a chance to chat.

For our expedition he wore a long visored cap, a shirt and jacket, blue jeans, and rubber boots (one of which leaked). He made the observation that regardless of arguments about the world military balance and competing ideologies, this was clearly an "American century" because in virtually every country blue jeans and T-shirts were the popular garb, especially among the youth, and U.S. fashions led the way in sports, music, cinema, and popular art styles.

One evening as we were strolling through shabby, unattractive Žagubica, the clear, crisp taste of a Montenegrin drink called Lozavača tingling in my mouth, I asked Djilas to tell me in his own words why he thought fishing had such special appeal to so many people. He said:

When I was twelve, a youngster in Montenegro, I watched a famous fisherman at work. That was 1923. I watched him fish with worms and both natural and artificial insects. He had a light rod and he also used frogs and live fish. He was a poor man seeking food but he also adored fishing. This was in the famous lake of Biogradsko Jezero.

He fished regularly there and also in some of the rivers of the region. He was our neighbor in the village of Podbišće: a poor peasant with a

little land near the river but it was bad, rocky land. And he was so desti-
tute that one of his boys died of hunger during the Austrian occupation of
World War I. He often said to me that if he didn't fish his family would
starve to death.

I became a passionate fisherman. We caught trout differently from you.
We didn't play them slowly. We had no reel to let out line. We just had a
little short line and jerked the fish out of the water so it fell on the grass
or in a tree. And we were very careful with our lines because it was hard
to find horses with long white tails with hair to braid.

Trout tastes marvelous. It is hard to catch. It is intelligent and it fights
well. There are many elements involved. In fishing, it is also important,
most important, to have a chance to dream and to think. Trout always
live in beautiful surroundings and clean cold water. I also find this stimu-
lating.

I think if I didn't fish with such enthusiasm I would not have broken
with the leadership. My thoughts became clarified as I fished. My individuality and integrity developed. Subconsciously I changed.

Also, as a writer, there was a change in me. My mind cleared away
unimportant thoughts. In this way I discovered and analysed many of the
motifs of my books. You are both active and inactive when you fish trout.
Part of the mind concentrates on finding and attracting and catching the
fish. But part of the mind is free to think original thoughts untarnished
by city life and modern complexities.

Perhaps one feels as prehistoric man felt. I feel I am doing what pre-
Slavic, Bronze Age and Stone Age people did. You go beyond civilization, before it. Maybe even the fisherman goes beyond and before man
himself.[3]

Djilas has written more than once of his love of fishing. In his
marvelous short story, "The Leper," he recalls scenes from the Tara
River, above which on a bluff stood the little house where he was
born, and in Biogradskoe Jezero, the beautiful lake set amidst a
primeval forest, where he often fished as a boy, after long hikes
from home, and where he fished again, with some success, on a
trip we made together in 1984. In "The Leper" he writes:

Noticing that the world outside was once more what it had been before,
a trout cautiously slipped down through the rapids to the depths of the
pool. Now it was quivering gently, ready to dart away but also ready to
lie at ease and jump lazily and cautiously at the files.

What did it think? What did it think of the world outside its pool, out
of the water? It lived unconscious of time, in a world that constantly of-

fered it the necessities of its life. But I had to fight for ideals, for a world different from the one that existed. What would be my fate if I should leave my world of struggle and ideals?[4]

Philosophically he observed in *Rise and Fall*:

I don't know how a man arrives at ideas and themes in art. They fit together out of his memories and observations, conversations and fantasies. I do know that with me it happened most often when I was out hunting or fishing—most spontaneously and abundantly when I was fishing for trout—and that it had something to do with the intense vigilance combined with half-conscious dreaming so characteristic of those moments. Dreaming, returning to some immemorial state of being, was more attractive to me than the sport itself and any success it might bring. But retreating into my inner solitude, I become inadvertently alienated from my comrades and from the reality they and I were creating.[5]

And, a final reflection:

Why do I like catching trout? I like to ponder and dream. But it's also because man is by nature a hunter; he began his life as a species by hunting and he always returns gladly and naturally to his primitive origins.

But why trout and not some other fish or some kind of game? Catching trout is a combination of sport and movement—swift currents, clear waters, the fish themselves shy and uncontrollable in all they do. They came into the rivers from some far-off world that no longer exists today, from seas of the Ice Age, as man, too, broke his way through from conditions that no longer exist today.

Catching trout is for intelligent, the most intelligent, people.[6]

It was certainly not the cruellest thing the regime did to punish Djilas when it excluded him from fishing but it was surely the most uselessly unkind. Fishing had nothing to do with ideological disputes or party discipline. To deprive a man already hard-pressed by prison, internal exile, discharge from high positions and unable to publish books in his own country was hard enough for a brilliant writer without depriving him of the pleasure he found in consorting with trout.

Political death is misery enough for such a man without the diabolical, sadistic footnote of banning him from all contact with trout. And maybe as a fisherman Milovan salvaged peace and tranquility from a stormy existence. Did not Confucius reflect: "Time spent in angling is not subtracted from a man's life"?

NOTES

1. Conversation with the Author beside a trout stream.
2. Ibid.
3. Ibid.
4. Djilas, Milovan. *The Leper and Other Stories*. New York: Harcourt, Brace and World, 1964, p. 47.
5. Djilas, Milovan. *Rise and Fall*. New York: Harcourt, Brace, Jovanovich, 1983, p. 68.
6. Djilas, Milovan. *Montenegro*. New York: Harcourt, Brace and World, 1962, p. 167.

3

Political Philosophy

Milovan Djilas is far better known as a Marxist (or, in truth, anti-Marxist) ideologue than as a writer in the literary sense. This is possibly Tito's last grim joke at the expense of a man who was his faithful acolyte and propagandist for almost twenty years. It is a grim joke, for Djilas evolved immensely as a person as well as political figure between 1941, when he first took arms as a member of Tito's Yugoslav Politburo and staged the military-political revolution in Montenegro, and during his later fight with Tito. Above all, as a writer he evolved.

Tito himself said he considered political death the "cruellest" death and ensured Milovan's ouster from the literary and political scene to accomplish such a "death."

When still a young man in his late twenties, Djilas embraced the Communist cause with much vigor and great enthusiasm, especially while Tito led the successful guerrilla resistance of World War II. At that time the goals of Stalin, Tito, and, on a lower echelon, Djilas, were seemingly identical. It still remained for Tito to stand up against the Soviet boss's errors and crass bullying. And it remained even longer for Djilas to carry Titoist rebellion to its logical conclusion aimed at overthrowing the bureaucratic "new class," which he "discovered" and analysed.

Djilas' reputation as a symbol of freedom is far less resonant in the world than that of Solzhenitsyn or of Sakharov. First of all, his independent attitude took shape in opposing the redoubtable Tito, who broke Communism loose from Stalin's control in 1948 and faced the Soviet dictator down. Tito, in other words, was a popular figure in the West, compared with the detested Stalin. Secondly, Djilas never had an international fame equivalent to the great Soviet author or the great Soviet physicist, both of whom were awarded Nobel prizes.

Djilas is an extremely fine writer, above all of short stories; yet when I was in Stockholm for the 1981 Nobel presentations and the president of the Swedish Academy conducted me through the Nobel library I asked to see what the card files had on "Djilas, Milovan." I found no book of his in any language; only reference to one magazine article on him by an ex-Communist author named Manes Sperber. Indirectly this anonymity clearly stemmed from the Tito muffler.

Djilas has become a kind of cult figure to specialists in Eastern European affairs. Perhaps as a result, most published references to him make him out as a somewhat turgid Marxist intellectual. He is much more than that. Indeed, his veins run red blood, not red ink; and his Muse is not Hegel or Marx but Montenegro, his birthland, and Njegoš, its poet. It is only an historical accident that his life coincided with the communization of East Europe instead of the endless wars between South Slavic chivalry and the Turks. His writing is not stale or doctrinaire but fresh, vigorous, and original; a poetic strain runs through it.

I shall seek to trace the logical steps by which the Stalin–Tito schism proceeded and to explain, primarily by selective use of Djilas' own words, not only why Tito's ideological revolt was necessary but also why it was both fated to succeed (as against Stalin) and also fated to fail (an event that has not yet occurred but is in the offing) because of Djilas.

His first ideological analysis, "The New Class," initially published in the United States (in 1957) soon gained an enormous worldwide success. This was in part because both Tito, the villain of the gladiatorial arena in Yugoslavia, and Djilas were romantic figures, their stories widely told in the folklore of World War II, and because it seemed astounding that the man who thumbed his nose at Stalin, and got away with it, should later be faced by the embarrassment of having one of his own leading lieutenants thumb his nose at him.

The Marshal's chosen revenge against his refractory aide was less the sentence of imprisonment that followed than the eventual condemnation to remain inside Yugoslavia but to have his books banned in his native land. As time elapsed, Djilas had discovered himself and found that he was more attached to the cause of literature than to the scientific analysis of Marxism. But since no author is as wholly understood in a foreign language as he is in his native tongue, the real Milovan Djilas was fated to remain at best little known, at worst unknown. Imagine if Pushkin's works had been available only in German or Hemingway's in Italian!

I have undertaken to try to rectify somewhat this injustice because I am an admirer of Djilas and a close friend and because I knew Tito rather better than most non-Yugoslavs and believe I can see with a special optic the problem of the dispute between these two men.

Milovan is deeply marked by his Montenegrin heritage although in appearance he belies the classic image of that doughty, immensely tall mountaineering race of warriors. Today, at 77, he is just over five feet ten inches tall, having shrunk more than an inch since his prime. He now weighs 178 pounds, perhaps two more than in his youth, and shows little sign of flabbiness. He is reputedly wholly without fear; despite the moodiness typical of this craggy people, he gives a cheerful impression and has a fine sense of humor; the corners of his mouth turn upward with smiles and there is a twinkle in his eyes. He is a thoughtful, philosophical man of notable and proven courage, both moral and physical.

His writing is replete with references to the pristine Montenegrin personality.

Vengeance . . . this is the breath of life one shares from the cradle with one's fellow clansmen, in both good fortune and bad, vengeance from eternity. Vengeance was the debt paid for the love and sacrifice our forebears and fellow clansmen bore for us.[1]

★★★

In Montenegro, where blows and abuse were considered grievous and unforgivable insults, it had been the custom to employ wet ropes, jack boots, and rifle butts in the interrogation of political offenders, to pull noses and mustaches, to curse fathers and grandfathers.[2]

In an analytical mood Milovan will describe his fellow countrymen as lazy, prone to pathetics, and often hysterical. They are surely given to uninhibited moodiness. Theirs is a male society. He speaks of an old peasant whose wife had produced a son who died at birth some thirty years earlier and after that only daughters, who do not tally when a Montenegrin compiles household records. The peasant said crudely of his old wife: "I planted seeds in her forty years and all in vain. No seed can sprout on rock and out of her you couldn't even get a stone." The daughters she bore him didn't count.

Yet with all his kindly chuckles at his countrymen's expense, Djilas is proud of Tennyson's tribute in a sonnet, "Montenegro,"which opens: "O smallest among peoples! rough rock-throne of Freedom!"

I first met Milovan during the final spring of World War II, on April 16, 1945, in Moscow, where he had come with Tito and a handful of other Yugoslavs to find out what Stalin's plans were for their country. At that moment, three weeks before the cease-fire in Europe, nobody doubted that Stalin was the only draughtsman for East European map-making, least of all the Yugoslavs, who had earned so much acclaim by their arduous and successful Communist resistance against the Axis powers.

I noted in my diary for that date: "Tito invited me to drink a few vodkas at a party with him and Marshal Budenny, a squat figure who was pouring it down between his handlebar mustachios. Tito introduced me to Milovan Djilas, the tough, moody Montenegrin who has attracted Stalin's attention by his reputation as a guerrilla and his ability to recite poetry. Djilas looked at me stonily and said: 'Ah, you are the American who writes that our Tito is slaughtering Serbian peasants with American rifles.' He turned his back. Tito chuckled, pounded me between the shoulders and said: 'Don't pay any attention to him.' "[3]

In September 1946 I drove a jeep from Rome to Athens, necessitating a traverse of Yugoslavia from north to south, and Djilas announced on Radio Belgrade that he would have me hanged as a friend of (Draža) Mihailović, the Royalist Četnik leader, if I came into the country. I came. Nothing happened. Djilas later wrote in his book *Rise and Fall*, "Sulzberger and I had long been antagonistic. On my part, it stemmed from his anti-Communism in the press; on his part, *he deserved to be hanged*."[4]

He added later to this ugly reminiscence, after I had unsuccessfully suggested Yugoslavia should liberate the imprisoned Archbishop Stepinac (later done): "Today Sulzberger and I are the best of friends. We look forward to fishing for trout together every summer, and to the rambling conversations shared by intellectuals who have grown old each with a distinctly different experience."[5]

In April 1951 I was in Belgrade and called on Djilas. I was on my way to Greece and Djilas asked if I would bear a message from Tito to King Paul and to General Grigoropoulos, chief of the Greek General Staff. This was startling when one considered that Yugoslavia had just been the Soviet Union's ally and that Greece was newly in NATO. The message was that Yugoslavia would be willing to join in mutual defense talks, perhaps an ultimate alliance?

I asked if this was Djilas' personal idea or if he spoke for Tito. "The latter," he said, looking me straight in the eye. "Very well," I said. "It's not my regular work but I'll transmit the message." I did, and the short-lived Balkan Pact of Yugoslavia, Greece, and Turkey ensued.

His last prison term came after he sent me proofs of *Conversations with Stalin* with a request that I write about it—which I did. He was then popped into jail. I relate the story of these earlier contacts in some detail because it demonstrates a rather odd background for prolonged amity.

On July 5, 1956, I had a good talk with Aneurin (Nye) Bevan, the leftwing English Socialist who knew and liked both Djilas and Tito. He told me he was furious with the Marshal because "he betrayed Djilas. He gave Djilas his approval to go ahead and write the articles published in the Yugoslav press and which later developed into *The New Class*. My wife [Jenny Lee] and I heard Tito give him his O.K. with our own ears. Tito doublecrossed him."

Six months later Jenny Lee told me: "Tito looks like a relative liberal compared to the other Communist leaders. He is working for a liberalization of the Soviet regime. Djilas is a mad Montenegrin poet. He showed no judgment at all in writing his opinions for the outside world." Another friend of Djilas, Stevan Dedijer, believes Djilas was too brutal and arrogant during the early days after Belgrade was liberated. But he greatly admires him now. One of Djilas' few friends told a group of British Labor party leaders, when visiting Belgrade, that he was suffering from the cold in his cell. The friend recommended to the visitors: "When you people win the next elections the first thing you had better do is put radiators in your prisons. You may need them later."

When I first met Djilas we spoke in limited Serbo-Croatian, which I knew slightly in a primitive way. (I spoke German with Tito.)

Subsequently, as Milovan's knowledge of French increased, that became the medium of our exchanges. Finally it was English in which he became fluent.

It is notable that Djilas is an exceptionally intelligent and equally disciplined man who taught himself Russian, French, and English in prison. Unfortunately for him he had more than sufficient time to spend in that unhappy classroom. But from childhood on he displayed an aptitude for self-education. This is one of many abilities I admire in Milovan (a name, incidentally, that few persons other than myself employ; his general nickname is Djido, used by family, friends, and those rare former Partisan or Party colleagues who still are bold enough to see him).

Blazing independence and immense capacity for self-sufficiency are traits I value greatly in Milovan and it is also one that has gotten him into a peck of trouble under different regimes. But Montenegrins have always been renowned for their spirit and their capacity to survive danger.

For a man of his years who has spent so long a time in desperate wartime battles and marches, in arduous jail cells and under great personal strain, he shows no scars of adversity. He is cheerful; his face betrays a readiness to laugh, and his mind is as eager for new ideas as that of a youth.

Thus both physically and mentally he was endowed by heritage to face up to a time of troubles. His native Montenegro is a cradle of liberty that was never entirely conquered by the ravaging Ottoman-Turkish Empire. His youthful education endowed him with a passion for the medieval folksongs and legends that have been handed down by his forefathers since the fourteenth century. University served as a highway to formal education but he was soon swept up into political agitation and prepared early for a lifetime of reflection—behind bars.

The ensuing period of peace—and personal peace and personal power—inspired within him the surprising trait (for a contemporary Marxist) of original cogitation with a heightened concern for the freedom of mankind, both personal and political liberty. Now that he has been condemned for the latter, by a disapproving regime, he fights off the political death of isolation from people and (until 1988) from Yugoslav book publishers, continuing to write for himself, to give form to his thoughts.

In demeanor Milovan is a quiet, gentle man in no way indicative of the turbulence he has displayed in both wartime and peacetime.

From the start he has been true to himself and his search for freedom, although the appearance of freedom's goal has changed vastly
for him since its youthful inspiration as a Marxist dream, which
was fated to turn sour. A line out of his novel *Montenegro* might
well be applied to his own personality rather than that of his ficti-
tious character, Janković: "God created me to live and enjoy myself
as a man, and to fight as a Serb; and I cannot do otherwise."[6] (The
Montenegrins consider themselves a particularly warlike branch of
the Serb people.)

As far as I can discern, Milovan harbors very little bitterness for
a man who has suffered so much from erstwhile friends. There are
many such, alas, among the companions who once admired, respected, and felt close to him and later deserted him when he needed
consolation. Now they fail even to recognize his existence when
they meet him in public by chance. Although he has been under
secret police observation and his telephone has been tapped since he
was last freed from prison, he brushes off as of little consequence
the "unremitting espionage against me."

Djilas today describes his political views rather broadly. In *The
Unperfect Society* he writes: "My past has not all been taken up with
revolution and violence; idealism and humanity are part of it too
. . . I have always felt myself a Yugoslav and a Serb, or, rather, a
Serb-Montenegrin. . . . From my earliest youth I have been an
adherent of socialism and never a social democrat. . . . My views
have never been, nor are they today, identical with those of the
social democrats."[7]

Djilas' literary ambition has been to write a truly great novel. In
my judgment he has so far failed in this despite published attempts.
But his political oeuvre and above all his magnificent short stories
are success enough. And if one can write brilliant short stories, like
Kipling and Hemingway, who can complain that their novels are
perhaps less wholly satisfying? Does one criticize Benvenuto Cellini
for not being Michelangelo?

NOTES

1. *Land Without Justice.* New York: Harcourt, Brace & Co., 1958, p. 107.
2. *Montenegro.* Op. cit., p. 34.
3. Sulzberger, C. L. *A Long Row of Candles.* New York: Macmillan,
1969, p. 16.
4. *Rise and Fall.* Op. cit., p. 259.

5. Ibid.

6. *Montenegro*. Op. cit.

7. Djilas, Milovan. *The Unperfect Society—Beyond the New Class*. London: Methuen and Co., 1969, p. 183.

4

Credo

Montenegro, in 1911, at the time of Djilas' birth and infancy, was dominated by two political ideas, freedom and union with Serbia. The little mountain country had liberated virtually all its own territory from the rival Turkish and Austrian empires but it was still ruled by an absolute monarchy that favored the idea of patriarchy. Nearby Serbia was a constitutional state with what appeared to be a relatively democratic rule and social system.

Thus, while all Montenegrins seemed to be engaged in a struggle for freedom, there was an almost Manichean dispute between those who favored a fully independent, liberalized Montenegro and those who worked for union with the Serbs into a South Slav nation. By the time Milovan was seven years old the latter had emerged in favor of an even greater Yugoslavia as a Federated Southern Slavdom.

On both sides of the Montenegrin debate the magic word was "freedom." Milovan consequently heard this word mentioned by everyone before he had even started primary school. It is therefore not surprising that his questing mind grasped at political concepts of even a rudimentary nature and came to favor "freedom" before he even knew what it was. As he matured the search for liberty changed. He was to conclude in a later book of a political nature: "Since man finds no peace in the cessation of ordeal, there can never be enough of struggle, victory and power."[1]

In his quest for the evanescent goal of freedom he has been led along paths of violence, intolerance, war, and revolution. His ultimate aims tended to vanish, but he resolved never to give up the pursuit, although "I have now reached a stage where I could spend my remaining days in the comfortable glow of being regarded as a rebel who endured, even as a morally triumphant one."[2]

In the end his ambitions for political influence were completely repressed by Tito. For a man with a determined interest in the improvement of human society, such a sentence was especially harsh. In Bled (May 7, 1954) Tito told me (Djilas was in jail): "We have forgotten him already";[3] that he had no influence and would never be allowed to rejoin the Communist Party, which he had voluntarily quit.

Djilas himself was subsequently to write: "However much I may secretly crave power, I hope with all my heart that this cup will pass from me and that I shall remain safely ensconced in the original toil-worn innocence of my ideas."[4] Later, with the passage of years, Milovan concluded: "A non-violent society is not a possibility."[5]

An eclectic doctrine was elaborated by Djilas in his exile from politics: "Everything that lives, everything that is human, falls not because it is rotten, but because it has been pushed by some new-born, new-tried force . . . ."[6]

"Revolution is not essential for victory over the Communist oligarchs and bureaucrats . . . civil wars are even less necessary. However, recourse should be had to all other forms of struggle—demonstrations, strikes, protest marches, protest resolutions, and the like, and, most important of all, open and courageous criticism and moral firmness."[7] In his isolated stage, Djilas was limited to only the last phrase of this outline: even his criticisms can be published only in foreign languages abroad.

The ideological evolution of Djilas was evident before his break with Tito and the Communist organization. While still Vice Premier charged with supervision of Central Committee affairs, he wrote in 1951: "From now on the party line is that there is no party line." As Fitzroy Maclean, head of Britain's wartime mission to Tito (1943–1944), was to write: "His views were always a little in advance of anybody else's."[8]

Djilas wrote (in 1953): "The Revolution cannot save itself by the past. It must find new ideas, new forms, a new appeal. . . . If it is to survive, the Revolution must transform itself into democracy and socialism." He asked Tito his opinion on these ideas published in the party organ and received the chief's answer: "They contain some things with which I do not agree. But in general they have many good points and I do not think that the other points are reason enough to stop you from writing. Go on writing."

That same year Djilas developed the odd idea (for a Communist propagandist) that he foresaw the emergence of "a new leftwing Socialist party," thus favoring a two-party system. Before being sent to prison in 1954 Djilas told a foreign journalist: "It will mean a lot for our country to have a citizen say what he thinks."[9]

Clearly what Djilas was tentatively advancing was the idea of a multi-party system in a state governed by a single monolithic party. Even he, later on, realized this idea could not make sense without a total overhaul of the political system—which he now favors. Lacking such a fundamental change he foresees continuation of the dead hand of bureaucracy, corrupted beyond escape.

Djilas today believes that one idea fully ousts and replaces another in the dynamics of social life. And he reminds his foreign readers: "I made my own decision according to my convictions, freely, insofar as a man can be free."[10] The qualification on his personal freedom clearly implies a belief in determinism. Linked to this is the recognition that "man has entered an electronic age supported by higher standards of education and immense advances in production."[11]

In a letter to me he acknowledges that his ideas are similar, if independently arrived at, to those of the American Zbigniew Brzezinski, who coined the phrase "technotronic society." He sees Communism "plunged into difficulties" by the new world trend. It must "pass out of the industrial stage, with the aid of electronics and massive education programs and the employment of skilled scientific workers, into a new and more complex age—the age of automation and mass production and mass consumption."[12]

Against this background of evolution he sees Marx as a scientist, especially in sociology, and an ideologist whose ideas and very existence seem to be withering.

It is interesting to note that in the generations succeeding Marx, most influential thinkers in countries following his creed have been Slavs: Lenin, Trotsky, Stalin, Bukharin, Tito, and heretics like Djilas, Sakharov, and even (although he would writhe with fury at seeing his name mentioned in the same phrase as these Communist leaders) the reactionary Solzhenitsyn. Naturally, Mao and his successors aren't remotely Slavic.

Concerning the growth in himself of disillusionment with Tito,

Milovan says that despite the years spent fighting the monarchy, there followed first a period of guerrilla warfare, then fairly soon afterward a denial of the cause for which he had fought. Djilas concludes philosophically:

Don't understand me wrongly. I don't think my life has been unhappy; I don't think that my life was tragic or difficult. I had difficulty as did other men, some in my condition, others under their own burden. I am not pessimistic, nor am I optimistic. If you mix optimism and pessimism I am a relatively normal person.

What we need is a vision of a new Yugoslavia, confederated in Western Europe. We need more free democratic forms. And, economically, Communism hasn't succeeded in either agriculture or industry. Industrial production is not efficient; there is too much bureaucracy and inflation. And corruption is very extensive in Yugoslavia. Many people are building weekend houses; where is the money coming from? There is no real equality. This is a stratified society. What is needed is more free ideas and free discussions to bring the needed changes.[13]

I asked what had changed him from a fanatically young Montenegrin underground Communist and Partisan leader to his present tolerant self. He replied:

I am a controversial person abroad. But I have been very logical in my development. I have always pursued absolute ideals like justice and freedom.

I rebelled first against Stalin, then against Tito. I always sought to improve things, to make things better, not dogmatically but in a pragmatic search for the ideal. My morality and my personality have not changed, only my ideas. I evolved slowly from Marxism toward democracy.

We have had enough revolutions, massacres, killings. Only counter-revolutionary elements favor violence nowadays, no others. So now I am a reformist, not a revolutionist. A reformist requests, argues, and what he achieves is consequently more permanent and more sensitive to changes and evolutions.

It is interesting that the most important Marxists today are the critics of communism. It is like the Protestant movement inside Catholicism: Marx and his theory and the Catholic church with its reformers—society is not coming closer to, but is moving further away from abolishing class differences.[14]

On March 24, 1959, Djilas jotted down in his diary: "Last night I dreamed a sentence word by word: 'Evil is when someone is the chief cook in his country but is not also the chief taster of what he cooks' . . . I do not believe in classless society, even though capitalism has heard the last bell toll for itself. Each future society will be a class one."[15]

He continues: "The contemporary world, which is becoming united through diversity and where each day science and art reveal anew the indefinable complexity of nature, society and man, will complete the decomposition of ideology, at least as we know it. This is the dramatic fate that awaits Communism which was once the most scientific ideology, the sole world ideology." In the Soviet Union after Stalin "the party bureaucracy learned that ideology is already unchangeable, that is, that it is dead . . . Communism must split apart and come into conflict on national grounds."[16]

In September 1984, during a discussion with me, Djilas maintained:

I think that a classless society would be possible, theoretically, only if mankind were perfect. Men are not perfect. Therefore such a society would be suitable only to angels or to robots.

At the end of my life I have concluded that ideas are the most important phenomena of human life. Man is basically, essentially, a creature with many characteristics but fundamentally he is a being with ideas. Even in everyday life Man cannot do anything without ideas. That means without some concrete form of intention or activity, of writing, of thinking, of working for an idea.

In the first period of my mature, crystallized thought I was a real believer in Communism. But in the second period, when my opposition to the regime developed, I started by disbelieving any idea that excluded a human struggle for better relations within a human society.

I learned that without ideas it's impossible to fight and live, but that all ideas and religions possess no absolute truth. Philosophical truth, political truth, is not definite, is not absolute. And from those conclusions I arrive at new approaches to society. Some sort of ideal society for humanity is impossible, for the reason that human beings are not ideal. If they were ideal they wouldn't be human beings.[17]

With respect to his own country he has become a sort of double heretic; against the regime and against the shape of his own personal idealism. He told me in 1972:

It is unrealistic to try and renew Marxism in the party. And you can't have a federation of Yugoslavia with factional divisions in the various parties.

There is *something* good in every philosophy, in every political teaching, even in every religion: something tending toward ideology and to the action connected with such thinking. But the only way humanity can protect itself against the wrong tenets of ideology, philosophy or religion is by a liberal, democratic, open society; the sole protection comes in a truly democratic form of government.[18]

He recognized that Communism was compelled by its own ideas and by realities in societies it wished to modify that "first it must wrest power." Power (*vlast*) is a key word in Djilas' political vocabulary. It is something he admired in those who initially held it, like Tito, but which corrupted those who held it. As he wrote in *The Unperfect Society*: "The Communists became so completely absorbed and engulfed in greed and the lust for power that their power became absolute, totalitarian; and in their struggle for power they showed themselves to be ordinary mortals, as fallible as other men."[19]

Excerpting Djilas' ideas from his later writings and from his conversations one can find, by piecing all together, the outline for a logical, cogent anti-Communism. Indeed, he argues that Communism no longer exists, as such; only anti-Communism in selected nations. And "Soviet Communism has become the mainstay of conservative Communist forces at home and abroad, while Yugoslav Communism is a model for the weakness and disintegration of Communism."[20]

Without even attempting to formulate a new ideology of his own, Djilas insists that any society must contain both a formal and informal opposition to its government and that this is a "vital necessity." Nations tend to shape the dogma they accept into their own image but "no nation has been prepared to lay down its life for the beauty of a dogma and no nation is going to find Communist dogma the exception."[21]

Djilas has carefully avoided at all times in his stormy career any temptation to confuse ideology with religion or to regard one as a substitute for the other. And he recognizes the immense importance of Communism before its apparent successes induced deformations and the decline he foresees. He acknowledges: "Marxism is the first real world ideology—i.e., one that has convulsed the whole human race in one way or another."[22]

But then, diverging from the Soviet dogma that is "international" (meaning pro-Soviet), he adds: "Communists consider nationalism as the deadliest sin, yet the irony is that, with the passing of time, nationalism has imposed itself as the surest way for Communists to enjoy the fruits of power—that greatest of all delights."[23]

Djilas is involved in a curious paradox. His personal quest for freedom condemned him at the start to shake off Communism and its restrictive bonds. At the same time Communism cannot exist with freedom, he reasons, arguing: "Any forms of freedom under Communism are bound to mean an end to the supremacy of Marxism as an ideology."[24]

The first step on that ideological byroad was Tito's. However, the Yugoslav dictator did not go any further along this path of deviation. Djilas did. He is still striding toward the end of the path, reasoning to himself: "It is impossible for a society under communism to extricate itself from the dead-end absurdities into which it has fallen."[25]

Put another way, he reasons: "Ideas are like vampires; ideas are capable of living after the death of the generations and social conditions in and by which they were inspired."[26]

In the simplest form one might say, following Djilas' argument: Nationalism must destroy the pretentions of universal Communism because men will die for their country but not for an abstract dogma; and freedom, in any form, once it enters a Communist system, eats into it and corrodes it fatally. He summarizes this formula accordingly: "Communist parties . . . are becoming . . . ideologically disunited and therefore more democratic, while the society they still dominate is becoming a democratic, stratified society."[27]

But Djilas always takes pains to make the point that religion is not an ideology and cannot substitute for or replace Communism, as many lazy thinkers believe. He argues: "Religions inspire and invigorate man above and beyond the potentiality he can find in himself or in the world outside him, but they cannot, in the modern world, change any particular society, because their aims and essence stretch above and beyond every society . . . Religions have, it is true, survived under Communism and are proving that they can outlast it, but they have not contributed any real criticism either of its ideology or of its practical aspects."[28]

He considers one of the most profound of Marx's conclusions (in *Das Kapital*) is that "the religious world is only a reflection of the real world." Over the years, Djilas concludes that, despite the disappearance of his own Marxist backgound with all the godlessness that went with it: "I became an even more confirmed atheist . . . from purely personal, ideological and existential reasons. I was not, nor am I today, one of those Communists who go back to their ancestral religion after having been disappointed with the realities of Communism."[29]

The lack of religion in his own make-up does not, as Djilas sees it, implicitly mean he has no faith. He has faith in his own humanity and that of mankind: "What I have learned and suffered is categorical; a man without faith, without ideas and ideals, can be imagined only as a man in a world of absolute void—the world of his own nonexistence." While discarding the legendary mysticism with which all religions adorn their divinity concepts, if anything he stresses the value of ethics with increased fervor. He sees his abandonment of even a vestigial Marxist belief as "a creative act."

Milovan, who is not above the delights of playing with paradox, says: "I think that basically I am a religious man who is an atheist at the same time, who started to be an atheist with the times." And he is convinced he once had a vision of Christ during the war: "I think I am basically a religious moral person in the religious sense. . . . During the struggle and the reading I did in prison I started to be an atheist, desite the Orthodox upbringing of my parents, who were never especially devout. That means I was never a particularly strong religious believer. But I think my nature is inclined to strong beliefs."[30]

Another time he told me: "Although I am not a religious man I think religion will exist as long as men exist." But he has no such prediction for Marxism and, because he respects Marx, he quotes with sly humor the prophet's own observations; "One thing is certain, I am not a Marxist."[31]

Djilas blames Communism for abetting rather than doing away with a class system; it has simply substituted its own bureaucratic hierarchy: "The party makes the class, but the class grows as a result and uses the party as a basis."[32] And this new class is made up of bureaucrats and exploiters, is voracious and insatiable, above all opposed to freedom. Yet "freedom" is the great goal of Milovan's life: his own freedom, his family's freedom, and freedom for his country and the society he lives in. He goes so far as to say: "Viewed from the standpoint of freedom, a military dictatorship in a Communist system would denote great progress. It would signify the termination of totalitarian party control, or of a party oligarchy."[33]

The fruits of revolution do not fall to the broad masses who participated in a revolution under party leadership. The bureaucracy garners the fruits; and "bureaucracy" means the party leadership that carried out the revolution.

In *The Unperfect Society* Djilas writes: "I am opposed to revolutionary means and the use of force in the struggle against Communism. Every Communist country has the right to defend itself." But the inherent strength in bureaucratic Communism "is power and it cannot survive indefinitely."

Djilas reviews his own intellectual revolt as follows: "After conflicts with Stalin I slowly developed in my own mind different ideas and critical thoughts about the Soviet Union; and of course I compared this Soviet experience with our own Yugoslav experience. I slowly developed point after point in different fields of political and social critiques of the Soviet system and of our own system."[34]

When I was overthrown in January 1954 they struck at me in every field, in private life and in intellectual life. I was completely boycotted by my own comrades with whom I had participated in the prewar period of the illegal party and during the war and after the war in the party and its activities. I saw the lack of justice existing in Communism and I continued to develop my ideas even more strongly, more radically. I published articles on my views in different magazines and newspapers before I was removed from power: different aspects of the same theme.

But I never came to the conclusion of Edvard Kardelj in my own country and Andrei Sakharov, the Soviet dissident, that idological convergence was bound to come about, convergence between West and East in a social and philosophical sense. I always disagreed. I don't believe in ideological and social convergence; only in scientific and technical convergence."[35]

I once asked him what dreams he had for his family, his country, himself, and he replied:

Not many hopes for myself. But I am absolutely convinced that this situation, this system as it is in Yugoslavia, cannot survive without reforms: democratic reforms. Otherwise it will lead toward catastrophic conflicts, cataclysmic internal conflicts which involve foreign powers, in the first place the Soviet Union and her satellites.

For my son I am hopeful because he is a moral and intelligent person. I believe that moral, intelligent persons always survive. As for myself, I am content with my situation as it is. Of course I have no great political ambition. I will help every man who participates in politics eagerly if he wishes to advance these beliefs. For myself, I am content to do nothing. I will continue with my literary work.

I don't believe that complete freedom, absolute freedom, is possible. Equality is not possible in human society. But revolutions have come about because of the belief in equality and in absolute freedom. And, of course, because the proper conditions for revolution had been created where it occurred.

Nobody can invent a revolution. The necessary conditions must first develop over a long period. Then revolution inspired by Utopian ideas can occur in certain existential conditions. Economic conditions—people must have enough food to eat and clothes to wear or that will be a necessary economic condition. But not only that. Moral conditions are also important. For example, if a society loses faith in its own values, that is also a presupposition, a requirement for revolution. The Communist system has turned into a corruption of the mind.[36]

As I understand Milovan's reasoning, he believes that a mixture of determinism and a yearning for freedom can best nourish any revolution that might erupt in a country where economic and social conditions have prepared the ground for change. But even after a successful revolution of this sort he wearily disbelieves in the possibility that man can attain true and complete freedom no matter how he tries—because he is human.

Having tried and to his later regret succeeded in helping a revolution take control in his own homeland, Milovan looks to literature for solace but this is largely a personal satisfaction he cannot share with many people in his native country.

For years I have argued with Djilas that his greatest, most real talent is as a fiction writer of short stories, and increasingly he has come to share my view. It began, he says, with "an aching, insatiable longing to be creative in literature" not just as an escape from political activity "but a genuine desire to bear witness to myself, regardless of where my real talent lay."

He admits he had come to realize that "literature for me is now more important than ideology or politics. I personally think that my vocation is more literary than political." This is certainly true; he has immense talent (that cannot be hidden in translation) and his short stories, above all, should be published in all literary languages. He himself adds regretfully (1984) that as a young man he sought to combine his two drives, literary and political; and this failed. He admitted: "My orientation toward writing is rising all the time; my political interests are smaller and smaller."

As he wrote in *Land Without Justice*: "One fights to achieve sacred dreams, and always plunders and lays waste along the way—to live in misery, in pain and death, but in one's thoughts to travel far. . . . Good poetry lasts, like anything else man snatches from eternity by work and intelligence. Man, the most beautiful poem of all, passes away quickly and is forgotten. But man has not yet sung the last of that poem. . . . It seems impossible in life to have something both useful and beautiful. So men are divided. Some are for the useful, some for the beautiful. I placed myself on the side of beauty."[37]

Although not religious in the usual sense of the word, religion deeply concerns Djilas and he admits that partially, in an intellectual sense but not emotionally, he is attracted.

As a Communist I did not repress my religious feelings but I was never truly religious. Probably there is some element of goodness in my character, my mentality, which is similar to religion. I believe in goodness and in humanity but this is not really a conscious religion at all.

I even noticed some religious facets in Tito. He was not a religious man but there were some things connected with the early religious upbringing he had in Croatia. He would never sign death penalties, I noticed. He ordered them but he never signed them! I think he felt it was a greater sin to sign a warrant than to order death by telephone or in a conversation. Some elements of childhood religion always stay. As the Polish philosopher Kilakowski said, Communism simply takes the place of unsuccessful religion in a man's soul.

Religion is a quality of a human being that will exist, unlike Marxism, so long as humanity exists. Human beings are inclined to believe in ideas, to be ideological, and I don't even differentiate much between ideas of religion and some ideological teachings. They are just different forms. It is even clear that Marx, in his early work, was inclined to certain religious teachings. For example, to create absolutely free men. He said that humans must in the end be humanized.[38]

Djilas says he has formulated a kind of "private philosophy which is still atheistic but is humanist and ethical."

I didn't evolve much as a person from my Communist youth until today. Maybe I am more moderate but also I am stricter and stronger than when I was a Communist. Not only on ethics, on political ideas. On human freedom and democracy. But I am less fanatical than when I was a Communist.

Man cannot live without some beliefs. This is the difference between humans and other creatures. When Aristotle said man was a political animal he was right. Some animals are also political and live in communities, organized communities. But only human beings are capable of producing or believing in ideas. Ideologies are something temporary. But religions are deeper, more eternal; relatively more eternal although not eternal in the absolute sense.

I cannot be religious because I simply don't believe in it and I think also that religion narrows the forms of life. Especially when an organized church teaches; and without a church of one or another sort there is no religion. Nobody would preach it or organize it. But religion is nearer than ideology, any ideology, to an essential need of human beings, the need for a spiritual aspect of life, some connection with eternity. This is the basis of religion and what churches use to reinforce their power.

Marxism, as an ideology, promises some kind of happy, Utopian future. But only for one generation after another. Communists don't look at eternity and they are not Utopian. Many democratic thinkers are more Utopian. They believe in improving human relations and even influencing the Soviet Union to be gentler, better, more democratic. They believe in peace, not violence. But I don't think democracy has an ideology. It is so broad that there is no definition.[39]

After many, many hours of conversation over a period of several years I have arrived at the conclusion that Djilas, unlike others who forsook the Communist "God that failed," has consolidated his position as he trod a strange and rather lonely middle way. He cannot practice religion because he doesn't believe it; he cannot practice Marxism because, by experience, he knows it all too well.

He is the man in the center, between two magnetic poles, condemned to the loneliness of an atheistic life of tolerance and freedom rather than the restricted Marxist doctrine of intolerance without freedom. He has discovered no new lovely and legendary credo but this lack does not impel him to resume a barren, restrictive life of dogma proven unworkable and untrue because man, a creature that covets freedom, cannot find it in Marx.

Once I asked: "It seems to me that if one looks at history, there are obviously bound to be further revolutions as new generations come along. What do you think should be the goal of the next revolution, the revolution of the children of today?"

"You mean in Communism?" he inquired.

"No, in the world. What should one seek to do? To achieve in the world of twenty years from now? We don't know what; complete freedom of all human beings or equal rights for human beings. There's sure to be a revolution, don't you think, in the future?" I asked.

"I don't think that complete freedom can ever come," he replied sadly.

"Man is the link between the eternal and the momentary, a moment of eternity. Man was and will be a fighter, according to the immutable law of his existence. . . . The results of each struggle, even the great ones, are temporary and inadequate to achieve the ideal. But the struggle alone in itself is great and creative. The struggle transforms itself into a myth, and people live by myths . . . "[40]

I asked him one day by the banks of the lazy river Mlava what he had concluded from his own agitated life were the meanings of life, of death, of love?

"Life has no aim," he remarked, somewhat sadly. "The unique aim of life is life itself. Of course men can invent meanings. Love is truly a form of such creation. As for death; it is simply natural for a human being. You see, if we don't die, new generations cannot come to life. Life and death, they form a part of each other."[41]

NOTES

1. *The Unperfect Society*. Op. cit., p. 165.
2. Ibid., pp. 171, 172.
3. *A Long Row of Candles*. Op. cit., p. 1007.
4. *The Unperfect Society*. Op. cit., p. 185.
5. Ibid.
6. Ibid.
7. Ibid., pp. 188, 189.
8. Maclean, Fitzroy. *Disputed Barricade*. London: JonathanCape, 1957, p. 145.
9. Djilas, Milovan. *The New Class—An Analysis of the Communist System*. New York: Frederick A. Praeger, 1957.
10. Ibid.
11. Ibid.
12. Letter to the Author.

13. Ibid.
14. Milenkovitch, M. and D. (eds.). *Parts of a Lifetime*. New York: Harcourt, Brace, Javanovich, 1980, p. 270.
15 Ibid.
16. Ibid.
17. Conversation with the Author, 1984.
18. Ibid.
19. *The Unperfect Society*. Op. cit., p. 10.
20. Ibid., p. 133.
21. Ibid.
22. Ibid, p. 42.
23. Ibid., p. 35.
24. Ibid., p. 102.
25. Ibid., p. 12.
26. Ibid., p. 37.
27. Ibid.
28. Ibid., pp. 26, 27.
29. Ibid., p. 24.
30. Conversation with the Author.
31. Marx's letter to F. A. Sorge, September 27, 1877.
32. *The New Class*. Op. cit., p. 40.
33. Ibid., p. 78.
34. Conversation with the Author, August, 1984.
35. Ibid.
36. Conversation with the Author, 1982.
37. *Land Without Justice*. Op. cit., pp. 23, 142.
38. Conversation with the Author, 1985.
39. Ibid.
40. Conversation with the Author, 1983.
41. Ibid.

5

Warrior

It is entirely proper that Milovan Djilas should have established for himself the reputation of fearless warrior during Tito's war against the Axis forces. He was, after all, a Montenegrin, descended from a fierce mountain people whose renown for fighting was enormous. Moreover, he came from a clan, the Vojnovići, whose very name derived from "warlike." His fame among his fellow Partisans for courage, ferocity, and stalwart demeanor was considerable.

Nevertheless, his military career was unusual, to say the least. By his own reckoning he is sure of only two men he personally killed in combat, despite his participation in desperate, bloody battles in some of which no quarter was given. And although he ended the war with the rank of colonel general, subordinate only to Marshal Tito, he never actually commanded any unit but led troops in battle more by personal example than by hierarchical discipline.

The only other rank he ever held in the Yugoslav army was lieutenant general. He was never a private or a proper soldier. And he was never a political commissar. He represented the Supreme Command, regardless of official grade, and in fact was as prestigious in a military sense whether he was wearing motley civilian clothes or his final uniform replete with general's tabs. He had not for a single moment been a soldier, strictly speaking. But he was always a warrior.

In June 1977, Djilas told me that since youth he had been "a very good shot" with a rifle. His grandfather and father were both officers in the tiny army of an independent Montenegro and, as a boy, he often swiped and used his father's gun; a nearby peasant taught him how to aim and fire it.

When our conversation turned to his military record he once admitted that during the war he had perforce been very tough and sometimes cruel. "Your soldiers don't respect you if you don't protect them," he said. "When they are ambushed or mistreated you have to take revenge on their behalf if you wish to keep commanding them." He acknowledged that he had for this reason often been forced to order executions—of prisoners or of miscreants.

There was no doubt in his mind that Germans died better than the people of any other nation; and he had also fought Italians, Serb nationalists, and Croat fascists. Most condemned men went to their death in a dream, stunned and overwhelmed. But often the Germans stood proudly and pointed at their hearts, stiffly erect and saying: "Here. Shoot here." He thought the Germans were the finest soldiers in the world but he had hated them: "Without hate you cannot fight a war." Yet he had come to conclude long after the shooting ceased that the Germans were indeed, as the Nazis proclaimed, the greatest representatives of the "white race."

I was interested to hear the concept of "race" from his lips; the only time I ever heard it. But he thought the Germans were better soldiers even than the British, although he admitted generously that the two successive leaders of the British military mission to Tito, Captain Bill Deakin and Brigadier Fitzroy Maclean, had been "extremely courageous and first class."[1]

Milovan cheerfully concedes that he was personally "a bad military commander. I knew nothing about warfare except I was a good shot. I used to practice shooting fish with my father's gun. And also I read a few theorists like Clausewitz. Instead, I generally was sent to take up desperate causes. And I almost always lost them," he adds with a grin.

I never was the commander of any unit but I participated in operations as the responsible person for the supreme command. For example, operations were prepared by the military commanders and they would ask me to approve or not, to make some observations. Thus, during the Fifth Offensive [the German Operation *Schwarz* designed to wipe out the Partisans in 1943] there was a question of whether we should leave the wounded behind our retreating troops or not. My decision was that our troops should stay with the wounded. And this was the reason at the end we were beaten, were destroyed.

That took place in June 1943 at Sutjeska. After I was overthrown and ousted from power I was criticized for this. But I said that we could not leave the wounded; there was no way out but to fight the Germans where we were. Even now I think I was right. Morally we were right.

I was a high party functionary and member of the staff. I was more a political leader, not military. But I was not the political commissar either. Maybe something like that, perhaps. In 1941, when the war started, our Yugoslav war, I didn't have any military rank. I was only a member of the Politburo of our Central Committee and member of the supreme command. I received my first rank in 1943; that means a little less than two years after our war began. My first rank was lieutenant general, I started no less than a general."[2]

Tito had decided to make each Politburo member a lieutenant general as well as his two best field commanders, Sreten Zujević and Arso Jovanović. As the war ended he promoted them one grade to colonel general. Tito was a great believer in hierarchical ranking, as can be seen in his own self-promotion to the grade of marshal, a far cry from his original status of simple soldier and then noncommissioned officer in the Hapsburg emperior's Austro-Hungarian army, as young Josip Broz, during World War I. Tito was always a formalist and vanity was his besetting sin. This led several among his intimate associates to murmur privately (they did not dare call him to account) about the way he started to appear in his photographs like a "Latin American dictator," a "Mexican general," or "Field Marshal Goering."

Djilas found that his own experience as a powerful Partisan leader, regardless of official grade, was of enormous importance in the process of his own self-education. He didn't learn much about soldiering in the sense of a normal military progression. Indeed, he admitted to me during a conversation at the famous battlefield of Sutjeska in 1984:

Now today I could not even be a commander of a regiment. I am not qualified. I might, of course, participate in some sort of political command. But nevertheless, I learned very much about war although it was more about general human conditions during a conflict. I mean about the attitudes of people, the morale of the soldiers, the conditions of a struggle. This, in essence, is really the political side of war; but I didn't learn much about the purely military side."[3]

Early on, during his Partisan experience, one of his Serbian colleagues said to him: "The Old Man [Tito] looks on our detachments as the future Red Army. No matter how broad and popular it may be, the revolution has to have its own army, even if it's a small one." (This was a political version of Mao Zedong's dictum: Power grows out of the barrel of a gun.)

He also learned a great deal about the psychological side, what it was like in battle. He says: "Something at the bottom of a man's memory tells him: a man becomes drunk, not even the most painful wounds hurt. A man finds himself different from his usual self, not himself at all. He becomes certain that he will survive, possessed with the urge to survive."[4]

Normally, Djilas recalls, he didn't carry a gun. On occasion he borrowed a weapon, as when he shot one of the two enemy soldiers he killed personally. But there were rare occasions when, on special missions, he was armed to the teeth. Thus he carried a rifle during a retreat southward from the main Partisan body when they were surrounded in 1943 and Tito ordered him to take forty men and protect the escape route of the principal force by a diversion. It was during the start of this maneuver that he and a comrade killed two Germans they encountered in the woods. They had to slay a pair of them quietly so their presence wasn't betrayed.

He wrote latter: "I unslung my rifle. Since I didn't dare fire again, because the Germans were some forty yards above—we could hear them shooting—I hit the German over the head. The rifle butt broke and he fell on his back. I pulled out my knife and with one motion slit his throat. I then handed the knife to Raja Nedeljković, whom I had known since before the war and whose village the Germans had massacred in 1941. Nedeljković stabbed the second German, who writhed but soon was still. This later gave rise to the story that I had slaughtered a German in hand-to-hand combat. Actually, like most prisoners, they were as if paralysed and didn't defend themselves or try to flee."[5]

Rather than a gun Djilas made it a point to carry with him always one book, "Gorski Vijenac" ("The Mountain Wreath"), a Serbian classic poem written by the Montenegrin Prince-Bishop Petar Petrović Njegoš, a nineteenth century ruler of the little state. This work was a great literary inspiration to Djilas, who later wrote a book on Njegoš. He recalls: "During the war, as in my illegal activities and in prison, I often felt fear, not only of torture and death, but at the thought that as a writer I might not have a chance to prove myself. If duty and the accomplishment of our aims required it, I faced danger."[6]

Milovan recollects that he killed only one other man personally. This was an Ustaši (Croatian–nationalist–facist) whom he shot in July 1942. The Ustaši was one of a formation the Partisans spotted at a distance. Milovan took the rifle of a Partisan soldier and shot the Croat at a range of about three hundred yards, missing with the first bullet but hitting him with two others. About this death he says:

I felt no chagrin. My grandfather and my ancestors had had similar events throughout their lives. I didn't regret that Ustaši. They were too brutal. But I later regretted that the German had to be killed; the one with the knife. Yet even he was a German from our German minority in the Vojvodina. I heard him and the other speaking Serbian before we fell on them. I hated them because they were traitors to their country, to Yugoslavia. Within a few minutes they died. We turned into the forest and marched on. By the time we got back to Tito's headquarters our little band had lost half its men; but we helped the main force to escape the enemy by delaying pursuit."[7]

Sutjeska is in splendid country: a rushing stream, tree–girt mountains, great sloping green fields, now including a museum and memorial of the battle with a mass common grave. While wandering around in 1984 Milovan made a curious confession for an avowed atheist: "One night, during our fight, in the river canyon, I had a distinct vision of Christ. I am sure that is what I saw. He looked like the Byzantine paintings and mosaics. I don't know why I saw the vision; or how it materialized."[8]

Tito was slightly wounded at Sutjeska by a German bomb fragment in the shoulder. Deakin, the British mission commander, was grazed by the same bomb.

The normal brutality of warfare is always increased in civil conflict and once again heightened by guerrilla or Partisan struggles. And Montenegro is cruel. In *Land Without Justice*, Milovan wrote: "This land was never one to reward virtue, but it has always been strong on taking revenge and punishing evil."[9]

The horror of the Partisan war against the Axis struck Milovan's own family sharply. His younger brother Milivoje was beaten in an enemy Četnik prison camp and then dragged off to be tortured. He answered all requests for information on Milovan and the partisans with "I won't talk" and "I wish to die honestly." He was tortured two months before being executed.

His older brother Aleksa was killed in 1941. His middle sister Dobrana was slaughtered by the Četniks, despite the fact that she was pregnant. The diabolical hatred between Serb nationalist Četniks and Yugoslav-minded Partisans was savage. Djilas recounts: "The Ustaši had selected twelve only sons from prominent Serbian families and killed them, while in the village of Miljevina they had slit the throats of Serbs over a vat—apparently so as to fill it with blood instead of fruit pulp. The Četniks had slaughtered groups of Moslems whom they tied together on the bridge over the Drina and threw into the river." [10]

Selective torture in the effort to extract battlefield information from prisoners was practiced by the Partisans, who were less exuberantly sadistic than the Četniks and Ustaši. But both sides engaged in the massacre of wounded and the execution of prisoners. Djilas writes that after they learned injured Partisans were butchered at Kraljevo Voda, "the massacre of the wounded was a decisive point in our dealings with the Germans; thereafter the Partisans gave the Germans measure for measure."

The horrors of the war possessed Djilas almost as vividly as they had possessed Goya during Napoleon's Peninsula campaign in Spain. He remembers, appalled: "We decided to deal severely with the Četniks: to burn down their houses and take no prisoners." [11] And he reports, aghast at the Croat fascists: "Young Ustaši had fun with the girls in this manner: when they shook hands with them during walks, they would place human ears, fingers or noses in their hands, just like village toughs who get a kick out of offering tobacco pouches with snakes in them." [12]

Protecting their own wounded became an obsessive question of high strategy with the Partisan command. In difficult situations, such as being completely surrounded by their enemies, Tito's generals were perplexed at the continual demand by their wounded that they be allowed to keep their weapons during attempts to break out from encircled positions from which it was most unlikely the casualties could be extricated. Djilas was deeply disturbed by the problem. Wounded could not be taken along during fierce breakouts. The wounded therefore, he eventually determined, had a moral right to protect themselves or to be in a position to commit suicide.

Djilas realized the responsibility for such a decision must be referred to Tito himself. He recalls that, after one battle for a breakout from encirclement, as a group of Partisans he led prepared hiding places for their wounded, who could not be brought along, one Serbian Partisan, minus a leg, said: "Don't worry about us, Comrade Djido. . . . You just break through. Only I beg you, let us keep our weapons." [13]

It was customary for the Germans and their allies to ferret out pockets of wounded with police dogs and slaughter them. This problem was acute during the Fifth Offensive, a series of battles against German, Italian, and Ustaši units in which the Partisans were outnumbered approximately seven to one and fought their way out of a narrow-mouthed sack about thirty miles in diameter.

One of the most difficult human problems faced by Tito and his commanders had to do with treatment of prisoners, an exceptionally arduous task for an army of guerrilla units constantly on the move and always seeking to avoid discovery from enemy scouts or aircraft. Djilas recounts that shortly after it became known that Germans, Četniks, and Ustaši were killing Partisans it was broadcast that the enemy would be treated in kind.

Their fighting men were summarily tried and sentenced by military courts or, in times of duress, executed on the spot. All Ustaši were sentenced to death after it was confirmed they were slitting the throats of captured Partisans. Djilas says the executions of prisoners were generally carried out by Montenegrin Partisans who volunteered for the job, anxious to avenge their comrades.

For a long while the Italians were treated more gently than their Axis allies, having avoided excesses of cruelty by their own units and having a special kind of Mediterranean rapport with their trans-Adriatic enemies. However, Tito's High Command resolved to execute Italians as well after one of Mussolini's men, a captive, had escaped from the Partisans and found his way back to his own side, with more than a little information. Djilas writes:

In that mortal struggle in which the Supreme Staff and all our units were engaged, the giving away of information became a grave matter, even if such information didn't reveal anything that the enemy didn't al-

ready know. Amid the death and destruction . . . moving stories reached
us: there were Partisans who wept as they executed the Italian prisoners,
with whom they had grown close in suffering and travail, even fondly
giving them Yugoslav nicknames.[14]

(The prisoners had been driven along together with their Partisan
captors, sharing the hardships and dangers of their embattled march.)

There is small doubt that the executions, whether of helpless enemies or Partisans who had violated orders or perpetrated severe infractions, such as desertion, were especially distasteful to Djilas, a
sensitive man who felt that it was sometimes necessary for him to
witness such grim occurrences. Once I asked him how often he had
been forced by the responsibility of his position as representative of
the Supreme Command to attend these sad events, so inevitable
among armies at war. How often had he been forced by his position to order that such executions should be carried out? "Several
times," he replied grimly to each question. "Several times," his lips
tight and his face drawn by the memory.

Was he not morally obliged to be present at executions he himself
had ordered? "No, I was not obliged to be present. But in a few
cases I was. In one or two cases I was obliged to attend in a political
capacity. Sentences had been openly publicized through the ranks
and the executions were done in full view of the army, drawn up
at attention."[15]

The executions were always done by firing squad commanded
by an officer. If it was evident the victim was not yet dead, after
the commander of the firing squad had checked, he generally ordered a second volley to be discharged. "Sometimes the officer shot
the victim in the head with a pistol."

Normally the firing squad aimed at the heart, the breast. Djilas
admitted to me that on the rare occasions when he witnessed executions, "I was always moved. But at the same time I controlled
myself in order not to show that I was affected."[16]

Public executions, in front of the army ranks, were ordered only
in instances where discipline had been "severely broken." But regardless of the violations, executions were always by firing squad.

Milovan's wartime experiences naturally involved his relations with
Tito and other officers and he observed the behavior under pressure
of the comrades he knew best. With Tito, whom he saw every day
unless he was off on a military or diplomatic assignment from the

marshal, a very special relationship developed. Almost a generation younger, all the Politburo members called Tito "Stari" (the old man), and Djilas remembers the easy familiarity, spiced by occasional irritations, that existed between him and his chief. "I was the only Central Committee member who ever openly disagreed with him," he says. "But I think he valued my sincerity."

Tito had a pretty young secretary known as "Zdenka" whose relationship was at least as important at night as during the daytime. Zdenka was skittish and quarrelsome and once Milovan lost his temper, screamed at her and warned he would throw her over a nearby cliff if she didn't shut up. Tito remained silent and other Politburo members were appalled. Zdenka, frightened, said no more.

Besides Tito, a few other leaders had similarly pretty young secretarial camp followers. Mitra Mitrović, his first wife, later observed to Milovan: "It goes with authority. In Serbia it is well known that a minister without his mistress is unthinkable."[17]

His wartime experience served Djilas well to fill his literary larder, both for novels and short stories he wrote in prison, with memory serving him in place of reference books. He learned a great deal about guerrilla warfare if virtually nothing about conventional military problems and maneuvers. He confesses that he soon realized that a Partisan group could only slow down an offensive mounted by a regular army, not defeat it. Thus he observed: "Guerrilla warfare means constant fighting rather than big battles. It is not spectacular victories and territories that count, but the annihilation of small units and the preservation of one's own vital force."

Moreover, as a leading Partisan told him, "The Old Man looks on our Partisan detachments as our future Red Army. The revolution had to have its own army, even if a small one."[18]

Although Djido's role as a Partisan commander, often in the field with fighting units, often at headquarters with Tito, was significant, it is strange that his former enemies don't mention him at all in their archives of World War II. The German archives at Freiburg don't even speak of him by name in all their extensive records. Archivists explain this may be because much of the documentation was destroyed before the war's end. The Italian archives in Rome don't refer to him in terms of the Montenegro fighting although Djilas organized and led the first Partisan resistance in occupied

Montenegro. Officials admit that the records are incomplete and disorganized.

Possibly this absence originates in the fact that Milovan's resistance role was more important politically than militarily; perhaps not.

NOTES

1. Conversation with the Author.
2. Ibid.
3. Ibid.
4. Ibid.
5. Djilas, Milovan. *Wartime*. London: Martin Secker and Warburg, Ltd., 1980, p. 283.
6. Ibid., p. 280.
7. Conversation with the Author.
8. Ibid.
9. *Land Without Justice*. Op. cit., p. 82.
10. *Wartime*. Op. cit., p. 139.
11. Ibid., p. 113.
12. Ibid., p. 211.
13. Ibid.
14. Ibid., p. 269.
15. Conversation with the Author.
16. Ibid.
17. Ibid.
18. *Wartime*. Op. cit., p. 81.

6

Prisoner

Victory in war brought freedom to Yugoslavia but not to Djilas. When Richard Lovelace, the 17th century English cavalier poet, wrote to his beloved Lucy Sacheverell from jail, he poetically assured her that "Stone walls do not a prison make nor iron bars a cage"; he could not foresee the fate of Milovan, an equally gifted writer on less fanciful subjects. Djilas passed a sixth of his life within hard stone walls and another even longer period encaged in Yugoslavia not by iron bars but by bureaucratic mandate refusing him permission to leave.

He was already adjudged an expert on the subject of prisons by Tito's own authority, Aleksandar Ranković, minister of Interior and boss of the Security Police, when in 1946, one year after the war, a meeting was called to discuss the construction of a new Belgrade Central Prison, Glavnica. All those at the conference were former "convicts" incarcerated by the monarchy. Expert advice was required. Milovan recalls:

That we had to have a new [central] jail was obvious, and no one argued the point. There were appeals to hygiene and humanity, but if the meeting had one keynote, it was this: on the outside, the new prison should resemble anything but a prison; on the inside, it should have none of those imperfections or "conveniences" that Communists had turned to advantage in their illegal prison communications back in prewar days. We would preclude any exchange of tapped messages by doubling the walls, and prevent notes or food from being pushed through the sewage pipes by building them with twists and bends. By providing for deep, insulated cellars, we would insure that the light of day would not penetrate to the cells and that no human voice calling from down there would ever be heard above. We would have windows of insulated glass set in concrete, which would look out on passageways, not on the outside world or the inner exercise courts. Finally, we envisioned a clean, wholesome prison, from the water supply and the toilets in every room to blankets and food preparation.

Work on the Central Jail was quickly begun. For speed and efficiency German prisoners were used as laborers, too. They had already earned such a reputation for diligence that tradesmen competed for their services all over Yugoslavia. As far as we were concerned, though, the Germans were simply workers carrying out our construction projects.[1]

A wry footnote to this grim civic project was sent me on August 23, 1977, by Milovan, in the form of a snapshot showing himself in prison garb during his initial royalist introduction to what was to become almost a way of life for him. The inscription on the picture read: "To C. L. Sulzberger. With friendship—this photo from prison 1936 because in my present prison of which I was one of the creators photography is forbidden. Milovan Djilas."

I have frequently talked with Milovan about the cruelties of imprisonment and what the experience can and does do to a man. He told me that in the pre-Communist government of the Crown he had been briefly held by police in 1932 and subsequently jailed from 1933 through April 1936; finally he was locked up for sixteen days in 1938 without being charged when he was picked up in a demonstration supporting Czechoslovakian freedom against Hitler during the summer of the Munich accord.

Milovan was a university undergraduate when first cast into a cell by the kingdom's worried authorities, who feared the spread of Communist ideas among the students. He remembers:

All of us were beaten but I was among those a little more heavily beaten because they knew me as relatively more active than some of the others. I was also held for three months in solitary confinement and again for two weeks because of "excessive resistance."

Solitary confinement in those days was particularly hard because you were mistreated in other ways, such as not being given enough food or like being kept awake at night with lights. I had nothing: no books, no nothing. I could not speak with anybody. It was strict isolation.

I spent time doing mental exercises and some physical exercise. We were allowed to walk outside twice a day for half an hour, without talking. But I walked a great deal in my cell. It now seems something like a joke but I estimated how far Moscow was from Belgrade and then counted the time before reaching Moscow by just walking in my cell.

Then I made it a practice to walk around my cell for several hours each day. I didn't have a watch nor a map but the clock in the prison chapel chimed regularly on the hour. I reckoned that I could safely count I covered four kilometers an hour—not the normal five—so I could be sure I would arrive in Moscow.[2]

This was a good way of passing time and keeping fit: five hours a day of steady trudging (plus the small amount of outdoor exercise prisoners were allowed together in the jail yard). In a sense, thereby, Milovan reached Moscow about ten years prior to his first actual visit as a special wartime envoy of Marshal Tito.

Each prisoner develops his own system of survival in solitary. The prisoner quickly separates himself from his own thinking, and begins communicating with "himself" as if "he" were a long-lost friend. With this splitting of his personality, a man begins a dialogue with himself. Peasants talk of harvests and cattle, intellectuals of philosophy.

One grows feverish from exaggerated empty thinking. Sudden laughter and sorrow overwhelm the prisoner when he runs into people again, as well as a feeling of shame because of all that thinking in which all things tend to become weightless. The prisoner welcomes every change: a new day carved into the wall, the knocking on the wall of a new neighbor, the arrival of the sentry to pick up laundry.[3]

★★★

I spent my time in jail concocting the most fantastic revolutionary schemes and adventures. Often I did it in installments; in between I thought of other things, but they were always secondary. While destroying me in one way, solitary confinement strengthened me in another: my belief in Communism, though in an unreal, dreamlike form.[4]

I asked him how he managed to retain his sanity. He replied:

Mental exercises. In the beginning I had no experience, how to think myself away from prison, how to escape its grip. My mind engaged in confused and complicated fantasies. But I saw this was tiring, that it was shallow and oppressive. Then I started to remember about my family, about my past, to combine people I then thought of with a future I imagined. That means, in prison, that the past, thinking about the past, is much better than thinking about the future. And the worst experience in prison is to fantasize. Do you understand me? That is the worst way for your mental sanity to survive in prison. With time I learned this.[5]

As a prisoner of the royal regime and when not in solitary, Djilas recalls that he was able to study and learn a great deal about Marxism and also about human beings. "In the first period I learned from books and from my comrades about the Communist Party and their revolutionary experiences in it. In that first period I started to be a real believer in Communism."[6]

Djilas was mentally and physically strong enough to benefit from the accumulated experience of rough adversity. The period served under the royal regime taught him, a young student, his own personal capacity for suffering. His character was annealed against hardship.

At first he was distinctly upset and even made a pretended suicide attempt with a penknife to persuade the police to end their bullying interrogation sessions with him. He was given ten days in the jail clinic.

That was his undergraduate course in the world of politically violent discord. The graduate course came some two decades later, long after the cause for which he first fought had carried him along on the crest of its wave to victory—and then that wave cast him to the side.

Djilas kept a diary on his thoughts and experiences; jottings like: "February 9, 1958: I have grown quite accustomed to life in a cell, and sometimes I even feel good. Is that the human power of adaptation?

"As I think back—I have been cold all my life. In primary school I was poorly dressed. In high school, the same. And I lived far from the school. At the university—not a single winter did I live in a room with heat (except for the last winter, when I slept on the cement floor in a steam-heated kitchen). In my first jail term I was cold. When it was over, I was still cold. Then came the war; and again it was cold."

Or: "January 21, 1959: Crime is undoubtedly a passion—a thirst for achievement, making up for some insufficiency, or inferiority— I am convinced that crime is part of the nature of man, and that in one measure or another it is true of every man. . . . All criminals are of a passionate, exalted nature . . . And criminals—even the greatest ones—are men like everyone else, with all human faults and good points, but many are without any moral criterion . . . ."[7]

He discovered his status was high among the peasant prisoners who recognized he was an educated man and "intellectual." The simple folk who shared facilities with him had been filled with propaganda tales by the experienced Marxists among the jailbirds. They boasted that life in Russia was prosperous and pleasant and that peasants there could use a miraculous machine into which wheat was poured at one end and spouted bread at the other.

Eventually Djilas was transferred from an underground cell in Glavnica, the police prison, to a new penitentiary on an island in the Sava River. It was known by the island's Turkish name, Ada Ciganlija. While he was there Mitra Mitrović, then his girlfriend, later his first wife, would come every Saturday and stand on the shore opposite wearing a bright red sweater so he could recognize her and read her affectionate thoughts even if he couldn't see her clearly enough to distinguish her features.

While at Ada Ciganlija, Milovan organized a hunger strike to protest the treatment of political prisoners like himself. He recalls: "A hunger strike is one of the toughest forms of struggle. Once the first few days are over, hunger becomes an intellectual awareness rather than an irresistible craving. The stomach has stopped functioning and the body has begun to draw on its own resources. Since man is the only creature aware of death, he can . . . curb his craving for life. One loses about a pound a day. . . . Having survived the first few days, one can easily go on until death, provided one has the courage."[8]

His career as a convict was principally divided between Sremska Mitrovica, a massive prison in Slavonia, near the border between Serbia and Croatia, and Lepoglava, an old converted monastery turned into prison under the Austro-Hungarian Empire. Lepoglava, which means "beautiful head," was especially renowned both under the Habsburgs and the Yugoslav ruling Karageorgević dynasty as the main site where political prisoners were incarcerated. The penitentiary had numerous solitary cells. Archbishop Stepinac, the Roman Catholic primate, was later held there during his lengthy sentence under Tito. The prisoners were generally allowed to eat together and Djilas there met Moše Pijade, who was to become a Djilas colleague in Tito's Politburo. Pijade was an intellectual whose writings were highly esteemed by the Communists and also a painter who spent all the time he could find in painting while serving his sentence. He had some talent and did a great many self-portraits.

Milovan remembers the monastery stronghold bitterly, saying: "We stayed there one year, until June 1935. When we rebelled we were all beaten by the guards. I was not beaten dangerously; several others had broken ribs. I only had a bad bruise where I was hit with a rifle butt. Soon I was returned to Sremska Mitrovica under tough conditions: tightly disciplined in walking, not allowed to speak. We were not permitted any contact."[9]

Because of his period of initiation under the Karageorgević jailers, Djilas knew better than to waste time when he was locked up again by his Communist comrades after he had complained of the "new class" of bureaucrats under Tito. During his prewar incarceration he set about studying French and Russian, in both of which he became fluent, and he even translated some of the works of Maxim Gorky. His thoughts were provoked by a continued "political re-education" that substituted for the Biblical "truth" learned as a schoolboy, which asserted that "a just life in this world prepares a man for the next."[10] He learned from Marxist dogma that "We were taught something far greater: to expect paradise in this world, not too far in the future."[11]

He was told that "there were two constants . . . the acceptance of the revolutionary Leninist side of Marxism and loyalty to the Soviet Union. . . . Marx, Engels, and Lenin were correct in everything they said and the purpose of our ideological study was to understand them as well as we possibly could. It wasn't until later years [before and during his Titoist incarceration] following the Moscow Trotskyist trials that Stalin was considered an absolute and undeniable authority and a major Marxist author. . . . We made subtle pronouncements: Marx was baroque, Lenin passionate and powerful, Stalin monumental."[12]

Djilas sought to escape the feeling of being cooped up away from his friends and family by writing occasional pieces including a short story and long poem. He kept a notebook containing observations on his fellow prisoners and prison life. He was startled to discover that many of his comrades were homosexuals and that almost without exception everyone practiced onanism.

When his term in Lepoglava ended he was sent back to Mitrovica where "the men were comforted by the rain, which eased their wounds, as we quickly approached the prison walls like ghosts."[13] His "gruesome" cell was near the one that was to hold him again after the war.

From there he wrote Mitra suggesting she forget ties of "bourgeois loyalty" to him for the sake of her own happiness, a recommendation she ignored. And in Sremska Mitrovica he had the opportunity to meet many leading Communists who accustomed him both to Party discipline and to personal intra-Party jealousies that blurred the prospects of an ultimate struggle for national power. He found prison a valuable laboratory for political life and concluded that Marxist theory strengthened him and gave him a feeling of courage. In April 1936 he was released.

By then he was a hardened, experienced veteran, accustomed to the cries and noise of beatings of Glavnica and to his own sufferings from police tortures in Sremska Mitrovica, many of which had been inherited from Turkish times. Of these he writes about his being bastinadoed as in the Ottoman regime.

I knelt down and stretched my arms in the back, and they tied my arms and feet securely with a chain and brought them together for a moment. Vujković [the torturer] tested the pizzle [dried ox penis attached to a baton]. Todor [another jailer] pushed me. I fell on my stomach, and as I fell the soles of my feet turned up. I could no longer stretch my legs, because the chain on my hands, tied behind my back, kept them bent. Nor could I wiggle them, because they were fastened around the ankles. He then leaped on my shoulders and stuffed a rag in my mouth . . .

I heard the gentle whistle of the pizzle and felt a sharp pain on the soles of my feet. The pain was sharper than I had expected. But it was now a familiar pain and I knew I would survive. It's the kind of pain that's transmitted directly to the brain: on the feet it feels like a cut with a knife, but even worse is the sharp reaction in the head. The body feels nothing. To each blow the victim responds with a scream, but the scream, stifled with a rag, turns into a painful grunt from the depths of one's intestines.

Finally I got angry and said I didn't want to talk. I clenched my teeth, determined not even to groan any more. They must have thought I had fainted. Vujković hit me a few more times and then stopped. He poured a bucket of water on my feet. I felt them burning, as if the water had come to a boil. They knew how to work with chains. They released them from my body in a split second. I rose and stumbled. My feet tingled, as if I were standing on hot sand. I don't know why—but I was crying, and tears kept flowing in spite of me.[14]

Another torment endured by Djilas:

That night I was tortured in a different way. [Kosmajac, a jailer,] was present, introducing into the proceedings a tone all his own, as if I had harmed him personally. He placed pencils between my toes and then squeezed them together. He pressed harder and harder, and looked as if he were going to burst. This seemingly innocent game caused extraordinary pain, which spread through my whole body. I suffered, I sweated, all over, and then released a howl so long and so loud that I was terrorized by it myself . . .

I also recall that I was now afraid they would hit me in the testicles rather than in the same spot repeatedly, which was what I had feared the night before. As if sensing this fear, Kosmajac hit me several times close to the testicles. I knew that a blow on the testicles wouldn't kill me, but I was afraid of a new permanent pain. There was no such blow. Instead, that animal, Kosmajac, rolled up my trouser leg and grabbed me by the testicles, and amid crude jokes and laughter about castrating all Communists he began squeezing and twisting them. It was a concentrated pain but all the more horrible as it then spread like an endless wave through the whole body and blocked out every other feeling, even the feeling of humiliation, which superseded all other feelings when the torture first started.[15]

Despite the psychological and physical horror in which they lived, the "political" prisoners, who were mostly young and entirely made up of leftists, managed to study Communism intensely and recruit new followers among the others confined with them. They formed study groups and individual sympathizers, with special knowledge, gave lectures to those whom they believed needed or qualified for Marxist training. Leninism-Stalinism was rapidly disseminated. The party organized its own hierarchy for the prison population and included many nationalists, who had no ideological training, among their new recruits.

Milovan once told me:

I really learned Marxism in prison. Sremska Mitrovica penitentiary before the war was my first "university" in Marxist rebelliousness. That is true for many Yugoslav Communists. We had Marxist books in prison and we had lectures and discussion groups every day. Even I, at the end of my imprisonment, had become one of the lecturers. I had only become a Party member in 1932, a few months before my arrest, and became secretary of the University Committee for the Party. But I had a lot to learn. I learned behind bars.[16]

Experience of anti–Communist brutality and of underground Communist organization and education proved invaluable to Djilas during his Titoist imprisonment. He remembers:

I lived in a cell with other prisoners. When I was in the cell, the guard all the time stayed in front of my door. In the period of my imprisonment from 1956 till 1961, I was twenty months in solitary.

They permitted me a daily walk, but along with the guard. And in both terms, I lived on one floor of one long building with more than 40 cells. This floor was isolated from the other parts of the building. And even when they sent some prisoners to live with me, they chose all killers who couldn't be used as workers, who were too old and some of them senile.

They were murderers. They were not bad people usually. All were peasants, some of them illiterate.

I was treated worse by the prewar regime. But under Tito's regime, I was more isolated. This is characteristic of both systems. For example, old Yugoslavia wasn't much interested in ideology, ideological discussions between prisoners. And spying between prisoners was not so totally organized as under the Tito regime. The Secret Police Chief of the prison called everyone of them and instructed them that if Djilas said something bad about the regime, the Socialists, Yugoslavia, or Tito, they would inform on me. This was nonsense, because I had no need to speak to such people about anything. We spoke about peasant life, generally.[17]

He made glum comparisons between the regimes that incarcerated him and their attitude to prisoners.

He was never given physical torture during his Titoist imprisonments and he was normally held in a large cell with criminal prisoners. But solitary confinement was frequent. He adds:

Psychologically and intellectually I was badly treated under the Communist regime. Conditions of food and medical treatment of prisoners were better than under the monarchy; however spying and discipline of prisoners were much, much worse under Tito.

All told, I spent about nine years in prison under the Communists. The cells were the same size as under the Karageorgevićs: about five meters long and three meters wide. Usually, when I was not in solitary, there were two or three people with me: not politicals; criminals, usually sentenced for embezzlement but often murders. The cells had barred windows. And they weren't heated; they were very cold. There was no water, no toilet. We used chamber pots and cleaned them. That was my duty. In the summer it was very hot and there were smelly insects. Lice. It was impossible to kill them all. It was an old building with many holes. The water we needed when we were thirsty we took back and forth in pots.

Today, I must say the guards are better people. Before the war they were brutal. They beat you with their fists even for minor infractions. Now they don't. They no longer do that. The police in this regime have always been correct with me. But the regime sought to break me with solitary confinements.

When I was first imprisoned by the Communist government in 1965 I worried because I regarded myself as a punished functionary and Central Committee member and it was hard to liquidate such ambitions and memories and erase them from my mind. But later I realized that from their point of view they had the right to jail even if that wasn't true from a juridical viewpoint. Such is the system, I saw, and I ceased to hate them. I said to myself: "No. Don't think bad things; just think fine things." And at once I started to change.

If, for example, I thought I had no perfect system to survive many years in prison, or if I thought Stefanija or my son might die, or something like that, I resolved to think the contrary and I found I was successful in this. And I discovered myself thinking that even I could survive not only prison but solitary confinement until the end of my life and keep myself surviving.[18]

As Milovan succeeded in shedding despair from his mind he decided to occupy himself in writing. He was allowed books but no writing materials. "Finally I was able to secure supplies of toilet paper. They tolerated this. And much of my translation of *Paradise Lost* was on toilet paper."

Djilas occupied himself at long length with the difficult task of translating John Milton's great work. It was an immensely arduous task. I have always been fascinated by Milovan's choice for a major translation and wondered if he saw some parallel between himself, fallen from power, and the angel Satan expelled from heaven. I think that rather than considering his own fate in relationship to that of Milton's Satan, Djilas secretly imagined Tito in that role, a figure whose vast talents and capacities were ruined by his evil weakness for self-aggrandizement, an inference that such was the weakness of the entire "new class" discerned by Djilas.

When I asked his reasons for choosing the Miltonian epic, Milovan replied: "I didn't know Milton's work well. I had only read part of it in an eighteenth century French prose translation. Being in prison I naturally thought of Milton's destiny because at the end he was also a revolutionary, disillusioned and even literally mad."[19] Milton, at first a royalist, had shifted enthusiastically to Cromwell's cause and was made to suffer for it by the Restoration government. That he was even approximately "mad" seems arguable.

Djilas continued his analysis:

This all was the personal side, my personal reasons for choosing *Paradise Lost*. Also, I thought that our language had no such important work and I was anxious to be the first to translate it into Serbian. I asked Stefanija to get a copy of the English text to me because my English is very imperfect. She did this very speedily with the help of an English friend and sent the volumes to me in prison. When I read Milton's first book, the start of *Paradise Lost*, I was naturally most enthusiastic and decided to try translating it. At the start it was very difficult but slowly I managed to work it into poetry. Of course, there were many mistakes in the beginning but when I left prison in 1956 I found a professor of English in Belgrade, a friend of Stefanija's, who helped me with the needed corrections. Of course the poetic rhythm is different but I have been told by literary professors that the translation is very correct.[20]

At this point Milovan added with regard to himself: "I never thought that I had lost some 'paradise' but I must admit that I find in Milton many elements with which I sympathize. For example, his intellectual psychology. And Satan's reasonings and actions. There are things in common with my own revolutionary past."[21]

(A sad epilogue to this story: the heartless regime, which has forbidden the publication inside Yugoslavia of anything written by Djilas, includes John Milton in the ban. The laborious, huge work isn't available in a Yugoslav library.[22])

It is certainly a cruel and stupid fate for a man who possesses great literary talent (which is not commonplace in Yugoslavia) to be so persecuted for his political opinions that every word he writes is subject, not to censorship, but to a complete ban, without any chance of reconsideration. Tito was quite right when he said "political death" is perhaps the worst form of reprisal.

To all intents and purposes Djilas has become a virtually forgotten man in his own country despite all he did on behalf of the regime that now governs it and despite a splendid record in the war that achieved liberation from the Germans. Even Milton, who defended the Cromwellian regicides and was harassed for this by Restoration authorities, escaped any menace of similar punishment.

One consequence of Djilas' difficulties with the regime and above all his prison sentences was that he lost most of his few remaining friends; almost all of them proved to be weak and disloyal. "They didn't remain friends," he says. "Even those who supported me at the beginning of my disagreement with the Central Committee. Even they faded away. Communists are not such courageous people when there is fighting taking place inside the party. They are only courageous against enemies; that means people who are wholly outside the movement. I wasn't in any conspiracy against the regime, against the party. I was simply an intellectual and moral rebel, discontented with the course of a patriotic leadership."[23]

His relations with the convicts he had come to know were on the whole amicable. He wrote of them in *The Unperfect Society*:

The murderers, for the most part vaporing old men, illiterate or barely literate, were the only human creatures with whom I had any contact that was not artificial, but such talk as we could exchange was always about the worries over their homes and their crops and village life, or about the wretched, petty everlasting and outrageous misfortunes of daily prison life.

They were all devout men, and I often asked myself: "What drives them to a belief in God? Is it possible for men to live without faith, without some sort of belief, without objectives or ideals?" They could not give me an answer, though there were a few honest and sharp-witted ones among them; for the rest, they were stupid, mean and treacherous men, and, moreover, lust for evil deeds in some had not been quenched by long years of hard labor and languishment. . . . While the younger prisoners were urged to give up their religion no one, and certainly none of the old men, was forbidden to say his prayers.[24]

In his introduction to *The Unperfect Society* Djilas wrote about his intellectual development in prison: "The quietude of my prison life, and my own tranquility, allowed ideas to ripen with self-assurance and without bitterness. I nurtured them, and I still nurture them, as the deepest revelation of all that I am and all that I aspire to achieve. . . . *The Unperfect Society* is the mature fruit of solitary and patient contemplation."

Once I asked Milovan if prison had not served as a sort of postgraduate university for him. He said:

I was more something like a monk in a monastery, in my cell. Of course I read very much. But I did not educate myself. I only learned English [which he mastered quite fluently]. And I wrote books, some of my books. I only wrote those which could not be suspected by prison officials. That is principally fiction.

The prison had a modest library. I received more from Stefanija, my wife. The officials usually were quite tolerant in this respect. I could even receive books in foreign languages. At first, until 1961, they gave me paper and ink. But later they were stricter. During my second term under the Tito regime they did not give me paper for three years until I threatened a new hunger strike just as a congress of the "Pen Club" was about to meet in Belgrade. It would have been a scandal if it became known I was striking. Then they gave me paper.[25]

I have often discussed with Milovan what extensive imprisonment does to a man:

Prison is good, but not for a long time. It is good if one is both a fighter and a thinking man. Isolation helps a man to analyse and correct his opinions. You have a chance to see truly what you are in the world and in society. Prison is a unique place in which a man can discover his own capabilities. Of course I speak of a strong, healthy man able to resist.

Before the war, in prison, I had finished my education as a Communist, both through books and through other prisoners. I became a dedicated fighter. During my first post-war term as a prisoner I deepened my opinions on mankind and destiny.

On the whole prison made me more courageous. I don't know why. I feel that now my existence in this world is completely mine, more than when I was a committed Communist. As a Communist I was a good fighter but I felt that I was not completely exercising my own personality. Now I live in my own world and I am happier than I was before.

Prison purified me. I am now a more sincere and open man. I may sin occasionally now but if I do I recognize and acknowledge that fact, the fact that I am sinful and not perfect. But twenty years ago I would have sinned and not admitted it even to myself.

Now I have certain very specific principles. I want good laws enacted and the privacy of every individual's life guaranteed. My principles nowadays are very precise. For we are still far, far from all the necessary freedoms and it will take a long time to achieve them.[26]

Another time he told me:

Prison exists in every man psychologically. To be alone, to be oppressed, to fight.

I feel guilty about my son. I feel responsible for going to prison when he was a small boy. But morally I had to go. When I went to prison, I thought about my son. I thought for him it would be better if I made a compromise by maneuvering my position. And the regime sent me a message suggesting a compromise but I refused. I see my conflict with my former comrades more as a conflict between spiritual thought and violent action than between two political ideas.[27]

In *The Unperfect Society* he deals with the psychological problems imposed upon him:

I find it almost impossible to describe the pain and distress I have suffered over the past fifteen years, particularly when I was in prison, as a result of my unsparing efforts to thrash out my ideas—pondering on their deeper meaning, their practicability and eventual outcome; thinking about the revolution, its promise and the aftermath, its enthusiasms and betrayals.

But no! It was not because I had sacrificed so much of the joy of life, and the literary creativity of my best years, to the teaching of ideas and to the revolution: these have been my greatest joy and my most perfect work. Something else was at stake: nothing less than the continuing existence of myself as myself . . . I spent . . . years cut off from most of the others, in the company of old men of varius nationalities and religions who were serving sentences for murder.[28]

The metempsychosis wrought by prison within himself is indicated by a brief exchange Milovan recounts: "A warden said to me once: 'You hate us.' I replied: 'No, I'm indifferent to you.' "[29]

When I asked Djilas, after he had completed his final sentence, what prison had done to him he summarized his thoughts accordingly:

Two years in prison is good. A long time is bad. It destroys the nerves. But it is not so bad for a political or spiritual man. You can test yourself and your own possibilities. War is serious as a testing power, but it is less complex. As a person you are alone in prison when you are in solitary confinement. You are not exposed to accidents as you are in a war.[30]

★★★

Suffering does not make a man more gentle, as Solzhenitsyn says. It provokes a man to violence and excess. Suffering rarely makes a man gentle.

The majority become more violent. But, as for me, now I am less interested in fighting. I am more interested in meditation than I was a few years ago.[31]

NOTES

1. *Rise and Fall*. Op. cit., pp. 3, 4.
2. Conversation with the Author.
3. Ibid.
4. *Memoir of a Revolutionary*. Djilas, Milovan. New York: Harcourt, Brace, Jovanovich, Inc. 1973, pp. 158, 159.
5. Conversation with the Author.
6. Ibid.
7. *Parts of a Lifetime*. Op. cit., pp. 280, 281.
8. *Memoir of a Revolutionary*. Op. cit., p. 222.
9. Conversation with the Author.
10. Ibid.
11. *Memoir of a Revolutionary*. Op. cit., p. 228.
12. Ibid., pp. 198, 199.
13. Ibid., p. 214.
14. Ibid., p. 121.
15. Ibid., pp. 158, 159.
16. Conversation with the Author.
17. Ibid.
18. Ibid.
19. Ibid.
20. Ibid.
21. Ibid.
22. Milton, Dzon. *Izgubljeni Raj*. Translated by Milovan Djilas. New York: Harcourt, Brace and World, 1969.
23. *The Unperfect Society*. Op. cit.
24. Ibid.
25. Conversation with the Author.
26. Conversation with the Author, August 1972.
27. Conversation with the Author.
28. *The Unperfect Society*. Op. cit., p. 15.
29. Ibid., p. 15.
30. Conversation with the Author.
31. Ibid.

7

Idols

In order to travel the road toward freedom it was necessary for Djilas first to shed two "gods," Josef Stalin and Josip Broz Tito. They were the twin idols before whose legendary altars he had worshipped in the contemporary manner of Biblical Ba'al. He determined to discard them completely, in succession, once he discovered that his gods, like others', had failed.

It is quite fascinating to see how an independent-minded, highly intelligent young man could be so attracted by the ideas and personalities of Stalin (before he had even met him) and Tito and then fall out so sharply with each.

In 1942, before he had encountered Stalin, Djilas wrote in the official Yugoslav Communist publication, *Borba*: "He is an epoch, the most crucial epoch in the history of mankind . . . It is a great honor to live in the era of Stalin, to fight under Stalin's leadership, which means to be a part of something that will live forever. Stalin is the thought, the spirit and the redemption of millions of ordinary people who are fighting for a better life. Through loving him the small become great, eternal, they become part of the eternal Stalin . . . ."[1]

By December 1944, the year he had first met Stalin, Djilas was able to write in *Borba*: "The behavior of Stalin, his entire personality, is so unaffected that it rapidly plunges a listener into the real, human world, into relations that are neither too intimate nor too cold, but simply human . . . Stalin is unusually modest, something that has already been written about many times. . . . He is, simply stated, a man, and that is more a man than most. From movements, humor and appearance to his brilliant theoretical and philosophical works, there is nothing discordant to him to upset the whole man . . . Stalin is a man simpler than anyone alive in the world today, and thus—an unsurpassable, magnificent genius of our time."[2]

It is startling, in view of this excessive adulation, to read Djilas' estimate of the same man in 1962 (*Conversations with Stalin*): "Every crime was possible to Stalin, for there was not one he had not committed. Whatever standards we use to take his measure, in any event—let us hope for all time to come—to him will fall the glory of being the greatest criminal in history. For in him was joined the criminal senselessness of Caligula with the refinement of a Borgia and the brutality of a Czar Ivan the Terrible."[3]

Djilas first detected blemishes in the Stalin image he had created for himself when the Soviet dictator, in their initial meeting, defended the crass behavior of his Red Army soldiers in Yugoslavia; then more doubts emerged when Stalin sought to trick Tito by inveigling him into an ill-considered union with Albania (which the Yugoslav avoided) and toying with Tito's appetite for Balkan prestige by luring him into dreams of a partnership with Bulgaria, in which Yugoslavia would have been senior partner. Finally, when fed up with Tito's refusal to play a subordinate, satellite role such as had been meted out by Moscow to the other East European nations, Stalin ousted Tito from the Cominform and the Soviet alliance system.

Stalin threatened with hostile military maneuvers on Yugoslavia's border, to frighten his obstinate junior partner, warning that with a wag of the finger he would do away with him.

The extraordinary aspect of the bickering twins, Stalin and Tito, each of whom sought to dismiss Djilas, was that Djilas at first venerated the two dictators as almost celestial beings. As a youthful Communist neophyte while still a university undergraduate, Djilas conceived an image of Stalin that endowed him with superhuman wisdom and the behavior of an infallible genius in every respect. Tito never attained that status in Milovan's concept of a political paradise, yet like Milton's Satan, Djilas was ousted from "Heaven" and condemned by Stalin for his insolence and unabashed behavior. Nevertheless, while standing stalwartly by Tito during the deadly quarrel with Moscow, Djilas never regarded him with any such awe as he bestowed upon the Soviet leader until the Marxist split in 1948.

As early as 1944 there were hints of a future anti-Soviet bias developing in Djilas' mind. When the irreparable schism came four years later, both Stalin and his lackey, Molotov, demanded that Djilas be expunged from the Belgrade leadership. This dire prominence in Stalin's mind almost certainly stemmed originally from Djilas' outspoken objections to barbaric behavior of Red Army soldiers in Yugoslavia. Milovan suggested to Tito that he be allowed to resign his positions to prevent a division with Moscow but Tito staunchly refused.

After Stalin's death Djilas' book *The New Class* was regarded by the Soviet leadership as a deadly poison somewhat similar in its argument to Trotsky's condemnation of bureaucratism in the Soviet Communist Party. In 1952, before Stalin's death, Djilas wounded him savagely by saying that Stalin's latterday ideas "resemble Trotsky's ideas more and more." This was accepted in about the same spirit Hitler might have shown were a Nazi writer to have compared him with the Zionist leader Chaim Weizmann.

It is appalling to view the zigzag impressions Djilas entertained of Stalin, the depth of the zags as contrasted with the height of the zigs. In an unpublished estimate written in 1969 Djilas summarized:

Although Stalin belongs among the greatest victors known to history, in fact he is one of the most defeated personalities. Above him there remains not a single lasting, unrenounced value. Victory transformed itself into defeat—of the person and the idea. What, then, is Stalin? Why is it that way?

In Stalin one can find all the characteristics of past tyrants. . . . But regardless of how much he resembles them, he is a new, original phenomenon . . . and although his oppression is the most perfidious and the most total, it seems to me that it would be not only oversimplified but also incorrect to view Stalin as a sadist or a criminal.

In Stalin's biography, Trotsky states that Stalin enjoyed watching animals being slaughtered, and Khrushchev in one place confirmed that, during his last years, Stalin suffered from paranoia. I do not know any facts that would either confirm or disprove their observations. Judging by everything, though, Stalin delighted in the execution of his opponents.

Etched in my memory forever is the expression that appeared on Stalin's face for a moment during a conference of the Yugoslav and Bulgarian delegations with Stalin and his colleagues on February 10, 1948, in the Kremlin. There was a cold and somber delight over the victim whose fate had already been sealed. . . . Stalin, even if we could not find criminal or maniac elements in him, nonetheless belongs among the most monstrous oppressors in history.[4]

In terms of Djilas' view of Stalin, early and late, the contrasts are endless. In 1944: "an unsurpassable, magnificent genius of our time."[5] In 1962: "the greatest criminal in history."[6]

Djilas knew Stalin better than most foreigners, but scarcely well, having met him only during his 1944/45 and 1947/48 trips to Moscow. He observed him with keen attention, as if he were the hawk-eyed newspaperman, Déon Lapčović, he used as an alias with false documents in Yugoslavia just before the German attack. But few people, and above all very few non-Russians, ever knew Stalin relatively "well"; those who did were either occasional diplomats, like America's Averell Harriman, who could speak to him on equal terms, or foreign Communists like Bulgaria's Georgi Dimitrov, the Comintern chief who could speak to him only as an acolyte.

Djilas' relationship with Tito was wholly different. He met him when he was very young and when Tito was an active, stout man in energetic middle age. Their friendship became very close, not simply on a political and then a wartime camaraderie basis but also a sort of father-and-son intimacy and even a kind of familiarity based on their differing ages as much as affection. Therefore Milovan's evaluation of Tito, especially in his book on him just after the great "heretic" died, was less extreme in favorable or unfavorable views than were his comments on Stalin, which truly ranged the full emotional gamut from pseudo-divinity to satanic.

There is no doubt that a warmth existed between the two Yugoslavs almost from the start and almost until the finish. Djilas knew Tito intimately, having shared day-to-day wartime routines, often lodgings, always the same harsh problems, and having survived the strains of such proximity with mutual respect, liking, and confidence. Indeed, Djilas ventured to disagree with Tito on occasion in Politburo or staff meetings and spoke up to him with a familiarity which none of his comrades ventured. Early on in his book *Tito*, published soon after the Yugoslav leader's death, he gave a balanced, clear appreciation, despite the accumulating differences between them.

I must admit that it was from Tito that I learned most about politics, not, to be sure, as one of the faithful, or even as his pupil. Through Tito, I discovered the essence of politics and political life. But I had opposing visions and aspirations. I sought an open society, personal freedom, and economic and political pluralism. I yearned for the power of law, not the law of power.[7]

In the above statement he extrapolates the theme of neo-bureaucracy emphasized in *The New Class* and applies it to the peak, Marshal Tito, of absolute power and multifarious palaces and properties. I personally doubt if his own preference for "the power of law" as contrasted with "the law of power" was so marked before 1948 and the rift with Stalin.

Djilas describes how Tito had been an excellent mechanic who ran machinery in prison and was familiar with agricultural tools and farming. But, except for the trade of metalworker in which he was trained, his knowledge seemed superficial.

Even Tito's knowledge of Marxism was meager. . . . He had picked up the "classics of Marxism" randomly—in prison, in Moscow party schools, which were rote sessions in which everyone declared his loyalty . . .

He was not an avid reader. . . . He danced nicely—a bit stiff, but elegantly—usually an old-fashioned waltz. Obviously Tito learned languages easily. After the war—or, rather, after the 1948 conflict with the Soviet Union—he mastered English well enough to be able to follow and grasp the simpler political texts. He had learned Russian as a prisoner during World War I, although it was apparent that he had never studied it thoroughly. . . . German was the foreign language in which he was most at home.[8]

Milovan did not grant that Tito had much soldierly talent and acknowledged he had "challenged both his military knowledge and his capabilities as a tactical commander" although the Marshal said he had been "a rigorous student of military strategy" in Moscow in the mid-1930s. Djilas comments that whatever formal knowledge Tito might claim, "he had no talent as a military leader."

Two personal weaknesses that Djilas detected in Tito and which he mentions time after time when writing about him were a taste for the vain trappings of life—uniforms, decorations and post-war estates and palaces—and a still more serious fault, referred to in frequent innuendos, that Tito showed an unusual interest in his own personal safety. This is as near as one can get to implying a man is a physical coward, without actually saying so. I have not heard this charge made about Tito by anyone else but it is worth repeating since Djilas was in a position to know and nobody could ever charge Milovan himself with a similar weakness.

He sums up Tito's principal characteristics as: "a strong sense of danger . . . an unconquerable will to live, to survive, and to endure; a shrewd and insatiable drive for power." Yet to these traits, Djilas adds:

His obsession with luxury, the pomp in Tito's character, grew all the more potent and elaborate as it fed on the consolidation of his personal character.

But singularity, whether real or simulated, does not preclude ostentation and vulgarity. Tito's appetite for luxury, for the fashionably acceptable, and his royal way of life and autocratic use of power were antiquated and degrading . . .

If Tito were to be subjected to doctrinal Communist scrutiny, he would stand condemned—as one of the most inconsistent and least Communist of rulers—more because of his royal way of life than for his autocratic way of governing.[9]

Djilas criticized Tito for choosing the prewar regent Prince Paul's White Palace, with its splendid porcelain and furniture and fine paintings, as his official office and residence where he could entertain state guests. At the same time he assailed him for taking over and greatly enlarging a nearby villa on the erstwhile "Rumunska" street (by then changed to Užicka) as a luxurious private home with magnificent gardens. He concludes:

Tito's predilection for luxury was inseparable from, though incidental to, his willful appropriation of palaces. . . . In the eyes of the people palaces are the seats and symbols of power. . . . Tito was never modest, never ordinary. Pomp was indispensable to him. It satisfied his strong *nouveau riche* instincts; it also compensated for his ideological deficiency, his inadequate education. Splendor was the visible and drastic expression not only of Tito's intentions and ambitions, but also of the development of the party and the government. During the war, his love of luxury and desire for power were strengthened after decisive bloody battles and legitimized by both a spontaneous and an organized popularization of Tito.[10]

With a touch of a sneer Djilas recounts:

Tito's court was in no way inferior to the royal court that had preceded it; in ostentation, it surpassed its predecessor. It was natural for Tito to

parade his jewelry, to indulge in pomp. It had nothing to do with his staff
or with protocol. His uniforms were edged with gold. Everything else
that he used had to be just right and very special. His belt buckle was
made out of pure gold, and was so heavy that it kept slipping down. He
wrote with a heavy gold pen. His chair was impressive and always placed
at the center of the room. . . . He used a sun lamp regularly to maintain
a tan. His teeth were false and gleaming white. . . . Collecting medals
for Tito was a high priority in state politics. . . . He held one of the
largest collections of medals in history.[11]

Tito's taste for grandeur, artificial barbering, decorations, and
splendid attire was by no means denigrated by most Yugoslavs. I
remember attending his pretentious reception for Khrushchev at the
Belgrade White Palace in 1955. When the stubby Russian boss wad-
dled into the luxurious apartments trailed by short, not notably
dressed members of his retinue, one of the tall, handsome followers
of Tito proudly murmured to me: "One would think they were the
Balkan peasants and we were the vast superpower." And he was
right.

Tito had four wives during his life; the second and third were
common-law marriages. All were pretty. At twenty-eight, in Siberia as a prisoner of war of the Czarist Russian government, he
married Pelagia Belousova, twelve years his junior, a beautiful
Communist girl who disappeared from his life after Tito was arrested in 1928. She returned to the Soviet Union and remarried.
Of their three children only one, the undistinguished Žarko, survived. His second wife was a Slovene Marxist girl named Hetta
Hass. He fathered another son by her, Aleksandar, and after they
separated during the war, she remarried. The third was his wartime
secretary Davorjanka Paunović (known as Zdenka), who was lovely.
She died in 1946 and was buried, by her wish, in the White Palace
(*Beli Dvor*), Tito's official residence.

His fourth wife, Jovanka, was also a striking beauty and twenty-
two years younger than Tito when he married her, a healthy, black-
haired Serbian girl. Tito's two sons, Žarko and Aleksandar (called
Miso), did not like her; but their relations with their father had
turned sour by that time. Jovanka hoped to have children with her
husband but he refused.

In comparing Tito with Stalin one may draw certain obvious
conclusions. Both were exceedingly vain but Stalin's vanity so ex-

ceeded human measurement that he could afford to give an impression of modesty to those who met him. He had no known desire for great splendor, did not lavish large sums on his dress or jewelry; in fact he never carried money with him and quite possibly had no real recollection of what it was worth. But until the very end, Stalin saw to it that the entire U.S.S.R. was adorned with larger-than-lifesize posters depicting him as a tall, solid-looking dignitary in full Marshal's uniform.

Right after World War II Tito allowed posters of his own photograph and slogans "We Want Tito" to be splattered around Yugoslavia but gradually this ostentatious conceit lessened. He was never even remotely so cruel a man, so sadistic as that super-brute Stalin. While the Soviet Union featured widespread and terrible purges of those thousands who disliked Stalin or whom he suspected of lukewarm support, Tito only indulged himself in one formal purge. In 1948, after his split with Moscow, while Yugoslavia was fighting for its life against the venomous threats of Cominform armies assembled against it, Tito decided to lock up all "Cominformists" on the bare, arid Adriatic island, Goli Otok.

My own judgment of Djilas' relationships with Stalin and Tito, his two great Communist "gods" who failed, is that he had a more romantic and passionate view of Stalin's mythical achievements and total greatness than he ever had of Tito's; yet he knew Tito far, far better and a vestige of the original affection and day-by-day admiration of wartime camaraderie remained with him to the end, although clouded with bitterness.

Thus Stalin was in truth a wholly artificial and superhuman creature of his prewar administration, a dream that became a nighmare. The impetus of such a regard carried Djilas on to a new crescendo of emotional adulation when he met Stalin for personal conversations in the 1940s, at the end of and after World War II. Yet he was alert enough to spot the dictator's resentment at his own contempt for Soviet soldiery brutalizing the Yugoslavs in 1944.

And he was even more sensitive, thereafter, when Stalin tried to make trouble for Tito in terms of his relations with the Balkan neighbor states, Albania and Bulgaria. Thus the ground had been prepared for the rift of 1948 and the psychological reaction of most Yugoslavs was loyalty to their own proven champion, Tito.

In terms of human judgments of the two greatest men, good or bad, he ever really knew, Djilas found himself too far from Stalin ever to evaluate the Soviet boss with any true accuracy concerning either his personal or political objectives; but he was too close to Tito to forgive him the shortcomings he had already started to discern before World War II's triumphant end.

Put another way, I cannot imagine Djilas surviving more than a maximum of one year's tolerance as a member of Stalin's court. The Georgian despot would certainly have invented the mythology excusing a purge of Milovan alone, had not the more grandiose scheme of a super-purge on a vaster scope already been invented by and for him through his own evil whims and his fawning idolators.

It is evident in Milovan's personality, background, and character that the weaknesses he found in Tito would especially offend him: hints of a lack in personal bravery (unimaginable to a Montenegrin warrior), signs of a love of pomp and splendor (unfamiliar to a poor, puritanical peasant boy). Regarding Djilas' view of his two friendly enemies: Tito was too close to him; the flaws showed. Stalin was too far from him; it required knowledge and acquaintance to understand his terrifying reality.

Djilas was influenced by many people during various phases of his life but he contends that no single or few particular influences predominated in the shaping of his character and personality. There is no doubt he felt a great emotional debt to Montenegro and to his ancestors, the Vojnović clan who dwelled in that craggy land.

My own impression, after numerous long conversations over a period of four decades, and after careful reading and re-reading of his nonfictional writing, is that the two men who most influenced his life and career remain Tito and Stalin, although he broke with both. And the man he met, if only briefly, whom he seemed most to admire as an individual was Churchill.

Milovan once recalled to me (and I quote from notes I jotted down at the time) that he had at first been "enormously impressed" by Stalin. Stalin had much charm, a sense of humor, an imposing presence. He was the greatest man of his time, greater than Churchill or Roosevelt, although Lenin was the greatest man of this century. Stalin's one weakness was "a fondness for eating."[12] The last is a curious and petty observation but might provide some clue for psychologists intent on analysing the Georgian's hidden personality.

When he came to write his astute book *Conversations with Stalin* after the tyrant's death, he penned an odd epitaph: "Viewed from the standpoint of success and political adroitness, Stalin is hardly surpassed by any statesman of his time. . . . Unsurpassed in violence and crime, Stalin was no less the leader and organizer of a certain social system. Today he rates very low, pilloried for his 'errors', through which the leaders of that same system seem intent to redeem both the system and themselves."

Initially an unabashed admirer, Djilas wound up with a mixed set of superlatives: "He knew that he was one of the cruelest, most despotic personalities in human history. But this did not worry him one bit, for he was convinced that he was executing the judgment of history."

Milovan was honored by invitation to a small supper at Stalin's country *dacha*, where only Molotov and "two or three high functionaries" were fellow guests. Everyone served himself from silver salvers on a sideboard. Djilas recalled that "we ate during a conversation which lasted five or six hours until daybreak . . . Stalin ate with gusto, but not greedily; the quantities of food he consumed were huge even for a large man. He drank moderately, slowly and carefully, unlike Molotov and particularly Beria." [13]

Stalin made several observations that deeply impressed the young Montenegrin. "This war is not as in the past," he said. "Whoever occupies a territory also imposes on it his own social system. Everyone imposes his own system as far as his army can reach." [14]

Later, after the Tito–Stalin quarrel broke into the open, Djilas, who stuck loyally by Tito, was to recall that the Yugoslavs had been liberated by their own Partisan army, not by Soviet troops as was the case with other Eastern European states. This helped to explain historically why there were such differences among the various forms of Communism that developed within them.

Also, he never forgot Stalin's cynical observations on Germany. "Some remarked that it would take the Germans more than fifty years to recover. Stalin observed, 'No, they will recover, and very quickly. Give them twelve to fifteen years and they'll be on their feet again. And this is why the unity of the Slavs is important.' " The Soviet boss then added grimly: "The war shall soon be over. [It was 1944 when the conversation took place.] We shall recover in fifteen or twenty years and then we'll have another go at it." [15]

Djilas gives a vivid portrait of Stalin:

He was not at all as you would expect from the pictures of him . . . his build is slightly below average . . . of very small stature and ungainly.

His torso was short and narrow, while his legs and arms are too long. . . . His left arm and shoulder seemed rather stiff. . . . He had quite a large paunch and his hair was sparse, though his scalp was not completely bald. . . . His face was white, with ruddy cheeks—a charcteristic of those who sit long hours in offices and known as the "Kremlin complexion". . . . His teeth were black and irregular, turned inward . . . Not even his mustache was thick or firm. Still the head was not a bad one; it had something of the folk, the peasantry, the *pater familias* about it—with those yellow eyes and a mixture of sternness and roguishness.

I was also surprised at his accent. One could tell that he was not a Russian. Nevertheless his Russian vocabulary was rich, and his manner of expression very vivid and plastic, and replete with Russian proverbs and sayings. As I later became convinced, Stalin was well acquainted with Russian literature—though only Russian—but the only real knowledge he had outside of Russian limits was his knowledge of political history . . .

It is engraved in my memory that Stalin used the term Russia, and not Soviet Union, which meant that he was not only inspiring Russian nationalism but was himself inspired by it and identified himself with it [although Stalin was a non-Slavic Georgian].[16]

It is evident that Djilas did not class Tito in the same grandiose category of men. Stalin was clearly wicked, for Djilas, but on a magnificently monstrous scale. Tito emerges as more human, with human faults and virtues.

He remembers his initial meeting with Tito after the latter had first come to Yugoslavia with Moscow's instructions to rebuild a shattered Communist Party. As always, throughout his acquaintance, Tito was dressed in a dandified, neat manner, a habit he kept up even during the heat of the arduous Partisan war. He recognized Tito operating as "Comrade Walther," from the Pijade jail portrait. He later wrote:

Tito exhibited nervousness, even rashness, in issuing commands. While he was confident in determining strategy that was more political than military in character, as a commander he reacted too quickly to the changes so inevitable in war, and as a result frequently changed his orders. Tempermental by nature, with an exceptional sense of danger and a keen, quick intelligence, in battle he didn't have the necessary detachment and often moved large units to protect himself and the Staff.[17]

There is a constant innuendo in Djilas' recollections to the effect that Tito was not physically brave and the implication lies under the statement that he moved units "to protect himself." I discussed this once in 1984 with Milovan during a trip to Montenegro. He said: "I think that in making political decisions, Tito like Stalin was very courageous. But privately, during the war, I saw many men more courageous than Tito. I cannot say that he was a coward."[18]

He asserts that Tito, unlike Stalin, was not a vindictive, vengeful man. His only brutality of a Stalinist nature was the establishment of the one concentration camp, Goli Otok.

Djilas had no use for Tito's vanity and love of splendor. I have often thought that the extreme unkindness with which Tito punished Djilas after the latter's excoriation of pompous, comfort-loving tendencies among the Yugoslav leaders and bureaucrats might have stemmed from personal resentment by the revolutionary boss whose bad example served implicitly to excuse similar behavior by his lieutenants. Djilas recounts:

Enjoying his role as leader, Tito would distribute cash gifts when making visits, most often to a children's home. Sreten Zujović, his frugal and energetic minister of finance, would grumble and mutter as he handed out fresh bank notes, and even Ranković privately criticized this practice.

Along with other sports, horse racing was resumed, and horses "from Marshal Tito's stable" made their appearance. Newspapers began to mention this stable in their racing sections. It was, in reality, a military stud farm belonging to the Guards. We had many troubles on that account, and many awkward questions: What if the horse from the Marshal's stable does not win? How come a Communist leader owns a stable anyway? And where do the earnings from this stable go? . . .

The train Tito used had formerly belonged to the Palace and was always kept in a special station (which had likewise once served the palace) in the Park at Topčider. High officials used to meet Tito there when he returned from a trip. Later the train was given more luxurious fittings . . . [19]

All of this of course was in the Stalin tradition, and modest in comparison with the immense wealth possessed and lavished by the Soviet tyrant. But the extent of corruption displayed by the Yugoslav leaders right after a crippling war appalled Djilas. He remembers: "Tito was not the only one ensconced in luxury and privilege though no one could match him. The rest of the top leaders . . . behaved similarly. A new ruling class was materializing spontaneously, systematically and along with it the inevitable envy and greed. The top leaders not only failed to halt the process, but themselves wallowed in privilege."[20]

It is thus clear that Djilas' admiration for Tito, which had been so pronounced before and during the Partisan war, was gradually diminished by his embarrassed discovery of clay feet attached to the idol.

One can compare Stalin and Tito, in Djilas' words:

To simplify the comparison between Tito and Stalin, Tito was a dictator, something like an autocratic leader; Stalin was an authoritarian boss. This is the difference. Tito insisted on strict adherence to the same ideology as himself but he was in many ways more tolerant than Stalin, if you compare the two. Stalin was something like an oriental, dark despot, strongly convinced in the rightness of his own opinions. Tito was like some sort of Western dictator, inclined to a good life personally but more human; by this very fact more human.

Stalin was really the creator of the Soviet Empire, not Lenin. Lenin was more of a spiritual founder, an intellectual and theoretical founder, but the real creator of the system was Stalin.[21]

Milovan seemed to enjoy the game of comparing Tito and Stalin. He wrote:

History does not know a despot as brutal and as cynical as Stalin was. He was methodical, all-embracing, and total as a criminal. . . . However, if we wish to determine what Stalin really means in the history of Communism, then he must for the present be regarded as being, next to Lenin, the most grandiose figure. He did not substantially develop the ideas of Communism but he championed them and brought them to realization in a society and a state. . . . He transformed backward Russia into an industrial power that is ever more resolutely and implacably aspiring to world mastery.[22]

He noted that Stalin was markedly a nationalist. This trait, seen in Stalin's use of the concept of Russian "fatherland" and even the Russian Orthodox Church during World War II as symbols to stir up popular support, continually played a role in Stalin's policymaking. Djilas cites this fundamental approach in discussing Stalin's Balkan policy, which often ran counter to Tito's, as in Bulgaria and Albania. What is more, Djilas reports that during a conversation in Moscow (1948) Stalin ordered cessation of foreign communist backing for the Greek regime in Athens. Djilas recalls Stalin saying:

Do you think that Britain and the United States—the United States, the strongest country in the world—will permit their arteries of communication in the Mediterranean to be severed? Nonsense! And we don't have a navy. The uprising in Greece must be wound up as soon as possible. . . . Greece is on a vital line of communications for the Western powers. The United States is directly involved there—the strongest country in the world.[23]

There Stalin was speaking as a Russian dictator rather than as an international revolutionary. If one carries Djilas' observations to their ultimate conclusion, one finds that the Tito–Stalin split was based more on nationalistic than dogmatic reasons, although dogma was gradually amended to suit the convenience of the nation states involved. And Djilas, too, became more of a nationalist.

Once when we were walking down to the river Tara Djilas summarized the whole question: "Tito was careful in treating his opponents. He avoided killing, ideological massacres, arbitrary proscription. He was not amoral; he had certain moral principles. Stalin was completely amoral. Tito made some mistakes but he was not an aggressor, like Stalin."[24]

The last of the great men Djilas encountered and who had some influence upon him, although only impressionistic, was Churchill. Milovan had already listened to Tito's admiring reports of his own meeting with the dauntless Englishman. The Yugoslav leader returned from that meeting making no secret of his admiration. When asked for his impression, Tito commented to his intimates: *"Vlast! Vlast! Vlast!* [Power]"

As recounted earlier, on his 1951 trip to London Djilas called on Churchill who was then chief of the opposition during a Labor government. He received Djilas one morning, still abed. He asked him if the Yugoslavs had been upset by the attack on them in his Fulton, Missouri (the "iron curtain") speech. "No," said Djilas. "We were pleased. It was a form of recognition." "No," said Churchill. "It was a mistake. But I have made many mistakes. I didn't think about them."[25] This admission greatly impressed Milovan.

For me the contrast between Djilas' flawed portraits of Tito and Stalin and unstinted admiration of Churchill mark stepping stones on his personal progress toward freedom.

It was only as a result of his recognition of the leaden oppressiveness of Stalin's dictatorship that he began to observe lesser but visible evidence inside Yugoslavia's regime of similar tendencies. Thus, both in a highly positive way and in a distinctly negative way, Stalin and Tito each figured large in influencing Milovan Djilas' career and life. Through these stern masters, unaware of their teaching, he learned that freedom cannot be rationed.

Djilas himself sees the negative role of those who influenced him. As a boy it was an Orthodox priest who "preached ethics very well" with the result that "this prompted me to turn toward Communism. I learned much from Tito but all the time I disagreed with him. I learned from him in the negative sense: more from what not to do than what to do." And finally: "Stalin also played a great role in my life. But it was more negative than positive. I cannot say that he played a decisive role in forming my person, my thoughts."[26]

He wrote in *The Unperfect Society* of *power*, which he occasionally was to dream of himself: "Once it has been savored, [it] poisons everyone with its lotus-like sweetness, divine or diabolic, or most probably a little of both."[27]

NOTES

1. *Borba*.
2. *Borba*.
3. Djilas, Milovan. *Conversations with Stalin*. New York: Harcourt, Brace and World, 1962.
4. *Parts of a Lifetime*. Op. cit., p. 320.
5. Ibid.
6. *Conversations with Stalin*. Op. cit.
7. Djilas, Milovan. *Wartime—With Tito and the Partisans*. London: Martin Secker and Warburg, 1977.
8. Ibid. (German was, of course, the official language of the Austrian Empire of Tito's youth.)
9. Ibid., p. 38.
10. Ibid., p. 96.
11. Ibid.
12. *Conversations with Stalin*. Op. cit.
13. Ibid., pp. 389, 390.
14. Ibid.
15. *Wartime with Tito*. Op. cit.
16. *Conversations with Stalin*. Op. cit., pp. 61, 62.
17. *Wartime with Tito*. Op. cit.

18. Conversation with the Author.

19. *Rise and Fall.* Op. cit., pp. 14, 15.

20. Ibid., p. 15.

21. Conversation with the Author, 1984.

22. *Conversations with Stalin.* Op. cit.

23. Ibid., p. 155.

24. Conversation with the Author.

25. This story was told to me by Djilas in Belgrade, May 18, 1968. *See*: Sulzberger, C. L. *An Age of Mediocrity* (New York: Macmillan, 1973), p. 431.

26. Conversation with the Author.

27. *The Unperfect Society.* Op. cit., p. 173.

Djilas' father, Nikola

Djilas while still in power after the war

Milovan and Stefica recently

Milovan at his birthplace (1984)

8

Intellectual

Once Djilas wrote me that "creative intellectuals and intellectuality are the most driving forces in humanity." There is no doubt that although in most respects self-educated, Milovan is both an intellectual and a creator. Indeed, thanks in part to the persecution he has suffered and the isolation he was forced to endure in prison, he is originally thoughtful and creative to the highest degree.

Intellectuality and creativity do not always go together. History is dotted with famous thinkers whose profound penetration of the problems of humankind in the Universe exceeded in quality and renown the originality of expression with which they sought to enlighten their fellow humans.

Djilas' intellectuality is by no means so profound as to bear comparison with that of Erasmus, for example; he is no true scholar despite his translation of Milton. Yet, as a writer, he has much influence and an insufficient reputation. *The New Class*, a trenchant observation on the ultimate destiny of Marx's theory of class structures, is widely read and admired. And the day will come when his short stories are elevated to their proper place in public esteem for admirable miniatures of fiction.

Of the many definitions given for "intellectual" by Webster's Third New International Dictionary (Unabridged), the two which seem to me most apt are: "A person devoted to matters of the mind and especially to the arts and letters" and "One given to study, reflection and speculation especially concerning large, profound, or abstract issues." These definitions, which refer quite clearly to application of external stimuli to natural intelligence in no sense require any profound initial book learning or formal education.

Milovan Djilas benefited from little early assistance in Webster's latter sense. After his Montenegrin years in primary and secondary school he stormed Belgrade University. There he was swiftly sucked into the vortex of an eager, leftist student body concerned far more with politics and ideology, often beyond the comprehension of that student body, than with the rote of learning.

Milovan delighted in this heady effusion of ideas, to a large degree consisting of but half-digested Marxism, and in a very brief time he had made himself the most active student revolutionist. This rush into the restless stream of idealized Marxism, which represented the broadest form of leaven surging through the corridors of various faculty buildings, giddily preoccupied the youthful Montenegrin.

Although enrolled as a literature major, Milovan studied philosophy as his main subject. He eargerly devoured Aristotle, Heraclitus, Epicurus, the 18th century French philosophers plus all the great German thinkers of the 19th century; and finally a hodgepodge of the early 20th century: Bergson, Lenin, Trotsky, William James, Bertrand Russell, Stalin.

His hunger for philosophical and ideological knowledge was all-consuming and his mischievous eye as an aspiring writer discovered fascinating quirks amid the turgid intellectual torrent. Thus he was amused that Engels was an industrialist with elegant manners and that Marx speculated in the stock market, not generally known by the Communist orthodoxy. These small details titillated the literary portion of Milovan's mind.

Milovan's university career was interrupted by arrest and incarceration. He was never awarded a degree, much to the regret of Stefanija, his second wife, who subsequently urged him: "You must have a faculty." After his final break with the Communist party and when he was, as it were, on his own and isolated, she suggested he complete his formal education; he demurred.

Milovan early considered himself a leftwing intellectual activist. Although still unaware what "ideology" meant to him he soon discovered the word had been coined by Antoine Louis Claude Destutt de Tracy, a French philosopher and former army officer who was a Senator under Napoleon and who published his theories as

"Eléments d'Idéologie." Napoleon used the term "ideologist" as a form of sarcasm. It was given respectability by Marx and Engels who employed it to group together types of moral, religious, and metaphysical thought.

Throughout his participation in active political affairs Djilas was a conscious and conscientious Marxist. He learned to occupy his spare time reading voraciously and relentlessly in an effort to inhale the limitless aura of creative thought that he had but tasted during his brief university career.

Notwithstanding, although Djilas never even completed the formal education to which he aspired, he became, by his own efforts, unusually cultivated, learned in philosophy, politics, literature, and art. He also made it a habit to look up whatever he did not understand.

Thus, Wolfgang Leonhard, an East German Marxist dissident and defector, told me: "Djilas was deeply fascinated by the idea that Yugoslav Communists were now evolving a brand new theory of a 'Managerial Revolution'. 'But Comrade Djilas,' I said to him, 'There's nothing new about that. It was also written by James Burnham fifteen years ago.' Djilas was astonished. He had never heard of Burnham. He immediately took down the name of his book and ordered five copies."[1]

This eagerness to learn new things and go to the bottom of old ideas marks Djilas as a genuine intellectual "given to study, reflection," and so on. At the same time he drove himself hungrily to acquire new knowledge; his creative urge responded to such nourishing.

In political theory he came to believe in Marx and a Serbian thinker, Vuk Karadžić; he still, although he has discarded the German's conclusions, knows Marx's works astonishingly well. He began their study in university and concluded it in a prison cell.

Incidentally, it is worth noting of his "Marxist" period that Djilas only read Trotsky relatively late in life and was more influenced by his personal example than by his doctrinal ideas. Recalling Trotsky's fate (murder by a Stalinist stooge), he thought it a more suitable end than Stalin's: "Better to be defeated and destroyed than to betray one's ideal; one's conscience."

His eagerness to create was always marked although this perforce came second to political revolution and its handmaiden, war, between the ages of twenty and forty. I once asked him if he had ever longed to use some other form than literature in order to express himself. He replied:

This is not known to anybody but as a young man, about sixteen or seventeen, I painted a little. I was inclined to painting without any doubt but not to music because my hearing is not first class. I have a good musical memory but my hearing is weak. I can play a *gusle* [single-stringed fiddle] but that is traditional. I learned from my father and my oldest brother. I am more concerned with literature than music.

And don't forget my poetry. In prison I counted and I found I had memorized between forty and fifty thousand lines of Serbian epic poetry! I also counted my knowledge of foreign poetry but it was not that large because I didn't read as much of it although I memorized well what I had learned.

I was certainly attracted to painting. None of my paintings exist now. They haven't survived. I remember I painted a dead man when I was in high school in Berane and who was given a famous funeral. I painted him in his coffin. I also painted the Biogradskoe Lake.[2]

Milovan is still extremely interested in painting and a faithful viewer of art exhibitions. He possesses two fine canvases of modern Yugoslav artists, the remarkably talented Lazar Vozarević and Leonid Sejka.

He never considered himself a war correspondent although, like Xenophon (author of the Anabasis) he was both a writer and a general. I once said to him: "Xenophon was probably the most famous war correspondent in history and you are the finest revolutionary stylist with whose work I am acquainted. Also, you know war." There is no doubt that Djilas' works contain much about fighting, destruction, and death, above all in his short stories and novels.

With his amazing memory, as demonstrated by the prodigious number of verses he managed to store in his mind and by his increasingly eager avidity for new learning, Milovan soon qualified for the term "intellectual." By the time he was sent to prison for the first time, he had made his mark and earned considerable admiration. He recalls: "The majority of philosophers with whose work I am acquainted I know from my post-war period of activity, long after university. Especially after 1948 I began systematically to read them."[3]

Certainly Milovan had been acclimatized psychologically to the

practical value of philosophical and intellectual learning as a means
to pragmatic political application. He recollects: "It was neither
Marxist literature nor the Communist movement which revealed to
me the path to Communism. . . . It was classical and humanistic
literature that drew me to Communism."[4]

Djilas has immense respect for intellectuals. He believes "The
role of the intellectual—the creative intellectual or the original
thinker—is decisive in society, every society. He inspires; he opens
up new long-range perspectives. In this respect it is of secondary
importance that usually such a thinker's ideas are not realized. Essentially the intellectual's importance is that he stimulates new forms
and new actions. I have in mind the intellectual who discovers the
currents of life; a human being is essentially the creature of ideas."[5]

The concept of "intellectual and intellectualism" is somewhat better
known and appreciated in Europe than in North America where
"intellectual" may often be a term of light dismissal for pedantic or
pretentious persons. On this subject Djilas feels:

I do not esteem intellectuals as a class. But I esteem individual, creative
intellectuals as those most important in the history of human development. And of course I include in this category the philosophers.

My own esthetic taste was and remains turned toward the classics. In
music my favorites have been Bach, Mozart, Beethoven, Rossini, Mous-
sorgsky, Borodin, Bizet, Stravinsky, Bartok.

My favorite painters are: Titian, Leonardo da Vinci, Goya, Manet,
Vlaminck, early Picasso.[6]

This is a cultivated but not audaciously experimental taste for a
European of Djilas' generation. But it is far more remarkable in
good judgment than it might seem offhand if one remembers that
Djilas was acquiring these solidly excellent critical views as a boy
in small Montenegrin towns, as a youth in Belgrade, where the art
museums are impoverished, and only brief subsequent sorties to the
outer world represented by Moscow, Paris, London, and New York.

Reviewing his fascination with Greek philosophers, Djilas adds,
"Plato was the writer, a great writer; he is a much more poetic man
with many philosophical sides to him. Aristotle displays only the
scientific method. Later, during my Marxist period after the war, I
came to prefer Heraclitus. And also Epicurus. Stalin told me he
considered Epicurus a great philosopher. But now I see that Aristotle can be ranked higher."[7]

To my mind it is not only fascinating that a poor peasant boy like Milovan, reared in a Spartan atmosphere, was illuminated by the same kind of epic poetry passed on from one generation to another as that which illuminated Homer; it is even more impressive that such origins were in no way allowed by Djilas to diminish his appetite for other cultural good taste. His eye for painting is shrewd, and existed before he ever saw his first old master. His avidity for philosophical stimulus endured from primitive highschool days into his old age, always seeking new thoughts and new directions for his dreams.

It is difficult to analyse with any confidence what portion of Djilas' excellent mind is devoted to absorbing thoughts, learning new ideas, and applying such concepts in a useful or pragmatic sense; and that portion which is simply exploding with the creative urge, ready to make use of all cerebral lessons with which it has been continually nourished since childhood. Whatever the case, it is beyond doubt that Milovan is representative of that pride in humanity vaunted by Shakespeare in *Comedy of Errors*: "Men, more divine, the masters of all these, Lords of the wide world and wild watery seas, imbued with *intellectual* sense . . . ."

As an author, a creative writer, Djilas' work can easily be divided into political or ideological works on the one hand, and romantic, fictional work on the other. The first group includes several books of which the best known is *The New Class*. This work brilliantly analysed Yugoslav Marxist experience in such a way that it could inevitably be extrapolated into a broader, catholic analysis showing how a class system anywhere contains the seeds of its own corruption. To my taste Djilas' novels are interesting if unsuccessful but his short stories are usually jewels.

The realism that showed so powerfully in his stories received considerable assistance from the material in the form of peasant tales, stories of love, death, rape, or murder that he heard from the "vaporing old" murderers with whom he occasionally shared a cell. He once told me: "In every one of my short stories there is something real. I believe that none of my stories was not founded on reality; but I added other elements to the basic facts."

Not many political leaders are particularly gifted authors but in this sense Milovan is unusual. Not only can he express his thoughts on governmental or ideological matters with great clarity and force, as in *The New Class*, but he has an extraordinary lucent gift in the purely literary sense. I classify him with the great short story writers of the last two centuries.

Two brief collections of tales, "The Leper" and "The Stone and the Violets," both available in English, contain true gems. He has not managed the longer form of novel with equal genius; but one cannot expect even so versatile a person as Djilas to have equally fine aptitudes in every field.

The Djilas stories are a tapestry of violence. Vindictive revenge rates high among the motivating forces of his vigorous, brutal, brave peasants, like Vuk, who belled a savage wolf so he starved because he frightened away potential game, or the marauding Serbian murderers of Backa. As an example of his pithy, accurate, and descriptive style I cite herewith quotations from two stories in "The Leper":

'Yes, alive, alive. Of course he's alive! I have learned where to hit him—straight between the eyes, but a little lower down, so that the bullet passes below his brain and does not kill him but stuns him. He must feel his death, the son of a bitch! What should death be if we did not feel it? And so,' he said as he went to shoveling the earth, 'I am burying him while he is still alive. Let him feel what it is like to die, how he ought to die!'[8]

***

In his deep-set greenish eyes and bristly mustaches could be seen a bitter spite and an entire absence of fear; this was even clearer in his words which were as rare as if they had been coined in gold and always harsh as a jagged saw cut.[9]

As an historian Djilas is a romanticist, influenced by Rousseau and by Kant's idealism. He is affected by the poetic sweep of Marx's attack on oppression and Dostoevsky's view of misery. In terms of logic he applies Marx's dialectical approach against Marx himself, and, in *The New Class*, *Land Without Justice*, and his essay "Tito," against the flaws in the world around him. His romanticism is confirmed by his approach to Njegoš and to Milton, whose Satan he seemingly regards as a revolutionary hero.

Milovan's career has been featured by a rivalry for his prior attention between politics and creative literature; although he believes he always preferred the latter he was forced by circumstance and also by the pressures of his conscience to favor the former. Yet he himself has written: "All through my life I have wanted to study literature or, more precisely, to write novels. And whenever (and that was frequently) I had to choose between the tasks assigned to me by the Central Committee and the party and the attempt to realize that desire to write, I 'denied' that urge." [10]

His entire life has thus been torn by conflicting interests: one caters to the revolutionary political leader and the other to the creative artist. The first seeks power and hopes to exercise it. The second abhors power and prefers seclusion for reflection and artistic creation, to engender thought and then to express it. The first seeks a stage on which to act; the second craves solitude. Djilas' life has been marked by a permanent internal contradiction. His creative urge was too strong to allow him total devotion to foster the events he sought; and his reflective, artistic side was inhibited and muzzled by the urge to promote events on the political horizon.

In terms of religion—and I treat these influences more in a literary, poetic, and musical sense of emotional art rather than intellectuality or devotion—his thoughts are difficult to specify. Once I remarked to him: "The only real impact of religion on your life is its ethic, as I understand it, not its legend; is that correct?" He replied: "I think this is true. For the simplest faith that is the exact expression. Probably the problem is also more complicated because literature, background, family ties, also influenced me."

His orthodox Christian heritage also left a mark. Djilas says:

I think it would not be correct to treat me as a religious man. Religion cannot replace Communism. The correct thing to say is that I am some sort of believer. But I don't believe in any religion and I don't feel any religions are individually more close to me than others.

Of course the Serbian Orthodox Christian Church influenced me in some spiritual way. Yet, philosophically, I feel although I don't know much about it that Buddhism is nearer to me, probably because Buddhism is very far from religion. It has no God; and probably this is the reason why I feel it is closer to me. [11]

Djilas started publishing short stories when he was a lad of seventeen in Montenegro, before he had left for Belgrade. He had a few poems printed later in the highbrow magazine *Misao* ("Thought") in 1931 and 1932, heavily sprinkled with reflections on Montenegro: "insatiable! You drain me, instead of the drop of rain, dreams, sun. . . . " "Land of my birth, dark, evil, painful, we are still thirsting for hate and love."

His style has varied with the subject matter but, in brief, it may be said that his political writing owes considerable literary method to the original works of Marx and Engels, both of whom were dextrous craftsmen, and his fictional narratives, short or long, are sensuously crafted and skillfully employ a musical language showing a predominant influence of Dostoevsky. However, it is interesting to note that when Milovan wrote me on the subject he omitted the great Russian's name and said: "My authors: Cervantes, Stendhal, Tolstoy, Homer, Melville, Hemingway, Gogol, Maupassant, Thomas Mann, Proust, Sophocles—and Vuk Karadžić [the modern reformer of the Serbian language]."[12]

I may point out another interesting oversight: whether consciously or by a simple lapse of memory he fails to note Njegoš, the greatest classical poet in the Serbian language. Yet both Dostoevsky and Njegoš belong on the list.

Petar II Njegoš was prince-bishop of Montenegro when it was an independent state ruled by Vladike (bishops) of the Petrović family of Njeguši, a feudal, theocratic system with each ruler appointing a nephew as his heir to be ratified by an assemblage of tribal chiefs. This primitive system was introduced by the Russian Czar Petar II. Njegoš wrote the impressive classical poem, *Gorski Vijenac* ("The Mountain Wreath"), which all Serbs and Montenegrins venerate.

Djilas produced one book on Njegoš and a novel, *Montenegro*. In his *Njegoš* (published in 1966), he writes exuberantly, even boastfully, of his great Montenegrin hero: "Being a Njegoš, from the first glimmer of consciousness Njegoš belonged not only to a proud and militant clan, but also to that bastion of Montenegro and its freedom—the Nahi" (administrative district) of Katuni. The Nahi of Katuni was for Montenegro the same beacon that Šumadija was for Serbia and the Piedmont was for Italy.

But it was also quite different from these. The Piedmont was a state, while Šumadija was a formation of free and nationalist peasants and merchants. The Nahi of Katuni was a collection of clans united solely by the struggle against the Turks, and then only somewhere from the seventeenth century on. The clans of Katuni were certainly among the first to refuse, or better to say, to persist in refusing to submit to the Turks . . . Once the men of Katuni broke away from the Turks—at the end of the seventeenth century—they were never to return to their sway.

Djilas justly points out that the clans of Katuni had an immense advantage over other groups of the Black Mountain area in that they were situated more closely than the rest of the clans to Venetian settlements around the magnificent Bay of Kotor; and Venice was still an Adriatic and Mediterranean power with whose strength the Turks, whose empire was beset by troubles, must perforce have had to reckon.

One reason for the strong and highly literate Slavic strain that runs through Djilas' nonpolitical writings is the combined influence of Njegoš' magnificent classic and of the remarkable collection of Serbian folklore epics built around the tale of the Battle of Kosovo in 1389. These were handed down generation after generation by successions of sightless poets, much like the minstrels who kept alive the Homeric tradition after the great Greek sat on the shore of his island home on Chios, peering darkly toward the narrow strait and the battered kingdom of Troy (today the Republic of Turkey).

Djilas says: "I think that my writing style has gone through different periods of change. In the first period, before the war, I was probably most influenced by Tolstoy. In my theoretical works after the war there was always in my style a mixture of Marx and our Serbian Karadzić. My *New Class* has been translated into more than forty languages, *Conversations with Stalin*, about twenty. And several other books in German and French although the first translation from Serbo-Croatian is almost always into English."

Venac, which specialized in encouraging young writers, published him sporadically while he was still in his teens. During his time at Belgrade University he started contributing to the literary journal *Misao* ("Thought"). *Misao* was conservative but had high standards of quality. Djilas' first contribution was a poem entitled "Mladic zvizduce nalazenje samog sebe" (A Young Man Whistles With Joy at Having Found Himself). This was an attempt at surrealism. *Politika*, the foremost newspaper in Yugoslavia, which paid much heed to cultural developments, printed several of his pieces that were what Djilas later termed "predominantly folkloristic in character."

I believe that the combination of Djilas' intellectuality, his appetite for all things cultural, and his amazing memory helped him enormously to bear the oppression and frequent solitude of prison life. For, as the best type of European "intellectual," he depended wholly on his own resources, with no secretary, no computer, and relatively limited library facilities.

What served as a motor for his mind was his greed for knowledge, which he managed easily to stuff into his brain and both digest and completely understand. This kind of self-sufficiency represented an invaluable psychological crutch, above all when joined to his courage and self-disciplined patience.

Djilas' conscious effort in his youth to produce surrealist writing reflects a fad among Yugoslav literary circles during the 1930s to ape this primarily French school. Koča Popović, another colonel general, who fought in the Spanish Civil War and later became Tito's chief of general staff, then foreign minister, had sought to make a name for himself as a young surrealist poet. Djilas wrote in 1937:

Surrealism sprang up in the jungle of postwar [World War I] literary movements. While the working class was opening the way to new [socialist] realism, intellectuals of the ruling class were moving even further away from reality and into ever deeper individualism. The earlier problems, more or less clear to everyone, gave way to obscurity of form, personal dreams and automatic texts as the negation of any art. In this process of negation surrealism behaved quite destructively and anarchistically . . .

Understood in this manner by surrealists themselves and by the rest of the normal world, surrealism is not even a pure literary movement. One could perhaps say that surrealism is a movement for the annihilation of art, for the annihilation of literature. In this respect there is also no doubt that surrealism passed through a certain evolution, evolving into the ultimate form of disintegration of bourgeois art . . .

The truth is that surrealism is a document of our times, an epoch of the most wonderful truths and the most hideous lies known to history . . . Whatever else it may be, surrealism is also a document of the inability of a culture in disintegration to create artistic works.[13]

Surrealism, as understood by young Yugoslav leftists like Djilas and Popović, had a social purpose (ignored by many more Western adherents of the cult) and allowed them to achieve both creative literary and social revolutionary goals; or, at least, to imagine they did so. For Milovan the surrrealist experiment enabled him to write creatively and simultaneously to act politically, the only time in his life he successfully managed this experiment (except, if you will, his political writings while editing the Communist organ *Borba*, or in *The New Class*).

The surrealist experiment, in terms of what he produced, does not appear to have been a triumph.

Djilas wrote in *Land Without Justice*, when his political future was already under a dark shadow: "Classical and humanistic literature did not lead directly to Communism, but taught more humane and just relations among men. Existing society, and particularly the political movements within it, were incapable even of promising this."

I must say this statement seems to be contradicted by Djilas himself when he says he was a Communist already in his late teens and even boasted that he had become one in high school (which I doubt). As a high school youth he read Gogol and enjoyed his social satire. At the age of twenty-one, before he was well-launched in his surprisingly deep classical education, he published in a magazine a satirical piece about bureaucracy that he entitled "Wheat, Wheat, Wheat." Years after that he became familiar with the works of Trotsky and their ideas on a "new class of owners and exploiters." Djilas acknowledges that Trotsky was "the first to criticize the system."

His jail diaries show how deeply he appreciated all the authors whose works he read there. In 1958 he writes: "These days I often think about Trotsky. I have finally decided that he is a very important figure and one that will grow more significant with time." But in the same period he finds Proust, an anti-ideologue if ever there was one, to be "a man of genius." And he discovers Hemingway "has a special talent."[14]

By May of 1958 he had so benefited by his prison reading and writing that "I feel so pleasant, almost as if I were not in jail . . . I am writing, I am working, and I am reaching out toward a new horizon . . . ." A few days later: "Political views and ideas are temporal. Artistic work is eternal." On June 28, he is re-reading Dostoevsky's *Idiot* and "I maintain that Dostoevsky is to be ranked with Shakespeare, Dante and Sophocles. In his own manner he is the greatest writer of all. And the one who, in my youth, and even now, attracted me the most. He and Shakespeare are the supreme poets."[15]

That October (1958) he concludes: "Man is the only being who is oriented toward eternity, and this is expressed most fully and most clearly by the fact that he creates artistic works as final, absolute values—fragments of eternity."[16]

He expresses admiration for Bertrand Russell and for Camus, different as they are, and concludes wistfully: "There is something incomparably beautiful in my imprisonment—in this internal peace, these reflections over my own conscience, my past, and the laws of human destiny." He quotes Goethe as saying somewhere that "the greatest evils for him were hope and fear." Milovan adds a sad personal note: "But it seems to me that the best thing for a failed man, especially one who has suffered defeats like mine, is for him to destroy hope. With it then he would destroy fear."[17]

He goes backward into time: "I am now reading the Bible. I never had time to read it before and I was always sorry that I did not have time to plow through this magnificent epic of the Jewish destiny. Now the opportunity is good and it fits into my plan for studying St. Basil of Ostrorog. I began with the story of Job and will browse through the rest."[18]

Both as a philosophic ideologue who found his own freedom in a prison and as a creator craving for inspiration, which he also discovered in the same prison, Djilas, alas, discovered the ideal graduate school in which, with his stern sense of discipline, he learned to appreciate and relish. A man who learns how to appreciate the value to himself of life behind bars is a true philosopher. As he wrote in his Jail Diary for July 20, 1958: "The only real and justified ideal of politics is freedom."[19]

NOTES

1. Conversation between the Author and Wolfgang Leonhard.
2. Conversation with the Author.
3. Ibid.
4. Ibid.
5. From a letter to the Author, January 17, 1985.
6. Ibid.
7. Conversation with the Author.
8. *The Leper and Other Stories.* Op. cit., p. 31.
9. Ibid.
10. *Legende o Njegosu.* Belgrade, 1952.
11. Conversation with the Author.
12. Ibid.

13. *Parts of a Lifetime.* Op. cit., pp. 99–101 (*Znanost i Zivot*, N. 5–6, 1937).

14. Ibid.

15. Ibid.

16. Ibid.

17. Ibid.

18. Ibid.

19. Ibid.

9

Heritage

Djilas is pure Montenegrin, a people noted for huge fightingmen and for an ability to survive difficult natural surroundings. Montenegro (Venetian dialect for "black mountain," the Slavic Crnagora) boasts that it was never conquered when Turkish armies overran east Europe from Athens to Vienna. Perhaps the Ottoman *bashibazouks* were disinclined to battle impoverished mountaineers for drab, barren settlements devoid of loot. Nevertheless freedom from tyrant or would-be conqueror has always been a Montenegrin goal. Milovan wrote in his novel *Montenegro*: "What we have not fought for we have not earned! The Montenegrin God is a God of vengeance—not just that, but that above all else."

The pre-Marxist Hegel wrote: "The history of the world is none other than the progress of the consciousness of freedom." If one substitutes "this man" for "the world," the German philosopher's phrase describes Djilas' life. Being a Montenegrin he was conceived in liberty. Liberty is rarely a gift to those who do not inherit it. It is born, not in the pain of others like human birth, but in the pain of those who seek it. That search by the Black Mountaineers was marked by horrendous violence. The turbulent streams running through their beautiful, jagged country should be tinged with blood. Since the first Slavic tribes swept southward to these Illyrian vastnesses, first fighting beak-nosed Albanians who called themselves "eagle-men" and then warding off successive Turkish incursions, brutal oppression contested the ceaseless urge for freedom stirring in the Montenegrin massif.

During the time of Djilas' grandparents, heads of decapitated prisoners were still affixed to the walls of conquered village fortresses; the screams of captives wailed over the hillsides as Turkish torturers, or the gypsies hired by them, administered the *bastinado* with dried bull pizzles attached to batons; flayed captives alive; amputated tongues; attached live men to butcher hooks—while black-clad women keened for their dead at night and combed and washed the hair on severed heads of those slain, even twirling their mustaches.

The Serbian race, and above all its most ferocious branch in Montenegro, has a peculiar pride in bloodshed. At the start of the 19th century a Bishop of Ochrid told a London lecture audience: "At the time when your William Shakespeare was writing his tragedies in ink we Serbian people were writing ours in blood."[1]

Milovan's father was of peasant stock. He ultimately became a career officer in the small Montenegrin army that helped neighboring forces expel the Turks from most of their Balkan possessions in 1912, when Milovan was a baby. From that year until 1918 Montenegro knew nothing but war—the first Balkan War, the second Balkan War, World War I. After the first world conflict ended, the little slavic state chose to join its big cousin Serbia in what eventually became Yugoslavia.

Montenegro had theretofore figured in the folk and epic poetry of southern Slavs, was much admired for its hardy spirit and legendary courage, and also served as the butt for affectionate jokes. Known for the vanity of its men—who included numerous six-foot-six-inch giants, and also for their sentimental adoration of Russia, the Great Slavic motherland, it was said that in 1914 when an Austro-Hungarian Imperial soldier warned his Montenegrin enemy across the border that war was coming, the Montenegrin commented: "We and the Russians can take care of you."

The belief was that Montenegrin males cared for little but fighting, drinking, and boasting, and were notoriously lazy in between. It is claimed one amiable soldier was riding a street car in Cetinje, the capital city, when the conductor asked him to move forward so that two schoolgirls could take the twin seat he vacated. "Had I wanted to walk," the grouchy man complained, "I wouldn't have bought a ticket."

The society of Montenegro is tradionally clannish. In this as well as several other respects, the Crnagora mountaineers resemble another doughty breed, the Scots, who shrugged off a partial British occupation and remained largely independent until their royal chieftains and those of England merged under the Stewarts. The Montenegrin Petrovići, Orovići, Poljani, and Vojnovići are the equivalent of the Scottish Camerons, Campbells, or MacDonalds. After Turkey overran prosperous areas some clans adapted Moslem lords.

In Montenegro's complex social structure the clan was subject to a larger tribal family. The custom of blood feud, with members of a family or clan sworn to avenge killings inflicted by another group, was the basic law. Tribal assemblies were empowered to adjudicate offenses against the blood code and eventually bring peace between sworn enemies. Ultimately, to tranquilize regional thirst for blood, the 19th century tribal rulers, bishops of the princely Njegoš family, set about suppressing the habit of vendetta—with only partial success.

Djilas speaks proudly of his clan, the Vojnovići, "a very old and very great clan." (*Vojnović* means "warrior.") His father, the officer, first fought in Vojnović feuds. At the time his father shot with them, the Vojnovići boasted 300 to 400 guns. This was a considerable portion of the private army of their tribe, the Zupjani, who mustered a thousand fighters. When Milovan was born in 1911 there were about sixteen tribes divided into clans.

"The psychology was very tribal," Milovan recounts. "A man was intimately connected with tribal life and could not imagine life outside. To be expelled was like ostracism in ancient Athens; a great punishment. But this has now changed. Expulsion is nothing. Tribal members or clan members emigrate elsewhere every day."[2]

The Djilas family was thus of the tribe Zupjan, the clan Vojnović. In the tribal seat, Zupa, there were several Vojnović houses and some of these belonged to the Djilasi. (*Djilas* means "leaper" or "jumper.") They boasted of great prestige and feudal wealth during the Middle Ages, claiming connection by marriage with the powerful Nemanjić dynasty that ruled medieval Serbia, the great South Slav kingdom. Milovan's nickname, "Djido," implies "nice guy" as well as "jumper" and also has connotations of "roughneck" and "joker."

Montenegro had been a minuscule independent state, boastfully pro-Russian, until 1918 when it was incorporated into the new South Slav country of Yugoslavia. Milovan was then seven years old. His earliest memories are tinged with vestiges of feudal and clannish traditions, memorialized in folk poetry and epics recited in the villages by blind bards, accompanying themselves on single-string fiddles.

Montenegro possesses little in the way of natural wealth. Its men are the tallest in Europe; its women, who wear black from their wedding to their grave, are patient and hard-working. The lovely tall daughter of King Nikola, last ruler of an independent Montenegrin state, was married off to Victor Emmanuel, Italy's gnomish sovereign.

When Milovan was a boy, Montenegro was famous for its magnificent landscape: rushing streams, high mountains whose igneous peaks glisten after being washed clean by storms; splendid forests and still lakes; placid nights echoing the snarl of wolves and the hoot of owls hunting beneath the bright stars.

Like other children of his generation, his primary education drew heavily upon the heroic tales recounted by local admirers. They hailed the Montenegrins as "Serbs," which is factual; the Montenegrin-Serb mountaineers of Southwest Yugoslavia speak the same language, use the same alphabet, and worship with the same rites as their Northeastern Serbian brothers. The songs and poems heard by the child Milovan vaunted: "Now, by your arms, the Serb sings again, and Serbdom flashes from your swords to the four corners of the earth . . . In the name of the Serb past you must conquer the future . . . ." But when union with Serbia came, many Montenegrins objected.

It may be seen that apart from impressive native intelligence, which Djido the "Leaper" presumably inherited from a peculiarly vigorous genetic mixture, violence was in his soul. And Milovan inherited, both through Mendelian genetic strains and Lamarckian acquired characteristics, a concept that was to guide him through life and which he described many years later: "The only real and justified ideal in politics is freedom." He and Hegel! He agreed with me that Montenegrins are "inherently rebellious by nature." Yet he had no illusions on the possibility that the Hegelian ideal of "freedom" as an ultimate aim of politics could be attained.

Milovan was born June 12, 1911, in Podbišće, a village on the Tara River near the border of Montenegro, still a minute kingdom on the frontier of Bosnia-Herzegovina, a partially Moslem area that had been annexed by the Habsburg emperor of Austria-Hungary. That imperial deed provoked Russian-inspired Serbian patriots to assassinate Vienna's crown prince Franz-Ferdinand in Sarajevo and thus light the spark for World War I.

Marko Djilas, Milovan's great granduncle, had been slain in a blood feud and the clannish obligation of revenge succeeded to Milovan's grandfather, Aleksa, who murdered the assassin. He was himself then cut down. King Nikola, last ruler of free Montenegro, appointed the survivor, Milovan's father, to his military cadet school in an effort to terminate this particular vendetta. Milovan recalled years later: "My first sight was of blood; my first words were bloody and bathed in blood."[3]

Milovan had three brothers and three sisters. Two other siblings died as infants. All seven survivors fought as Communist partisans in World War II; three were slain. And his old father was murdered after the war by two Albanians in the village of Srbica, near Kosovo.

His childhood was austere but the family was held together by the quiet strength of the mother, a wise and moral woman. The father of the family was an admirer of King Nikola but he swung his allegiance to Yugoslavia when Montenegro was absorbed into the South Slav federated state.

Their house on a hillside above the Tara was modest: an upper floor contained four small rooms including a kitchen and a storehouse for food where cheeses were prepared. One was a sitting room. Another, upstairs, was an attic where meat was smoked. Two rooms were used for sleeping but there was only one bed; for the father. The rest of the family curled up on the floor on mattresses covered by blankets.

Reminiscing, as we stood on the threshold of his birthplace years later, Milovan recalls: "When I was a boy this was a relatively high standard for my district in Montenegro. Now there is a better life. We only had meat twice a summer but every day in winter. That meant we were prosperous."[4]

He concedes that he was a mischievous child. He enjoyed youthful tricks like setting his father's store of rifle cartridges alight with embers from the hearth. "My mother beat me hardest of all," he says ruefully. "Years later, when she was over eighty, she told me she regretted having been so tough with me." He displayed a picture of the poor woman, her long, solemn, strong face framed by a black shawl.

"I was born around five o'clock in the afternoon in the down-stairs part of the house [the barn] where my mother had gone when she had the first pains because she was ashamed. I went to school at the age of six. This was earlier than most boys because my mother insisted. She said: 'Let's send him to school so the house can be quiet. I cannot put up with him. He is difficult.' But I was the best in the school. I went on to primary school and then gymnasium [secondary school] in Kolašin and Berane. I finished gymnasium at eighteen."[5]

In 1984 Milovan guided me around Podbišće and Mojkovac, the neighboring village, which his father, then a Montenegrin major, had liberated from Turkish control in 1916. We visited the graves of his parents. Milovan, who had designed the headstones and who paid for the upkeep of the small cemetery, was overcome with emotion.

We motored on to nearby Bijelo Polje and he pointed out the house where his brother Aleksa had been shot down by a Četnik ambush during the war. His younger brother, Milivoje, was tortured to death by police of the collaborationist government during the occupation. One brother, Akim, survives.

As we drove away Milovan cheered himself by recounting a story he had told Stalin in Moscow: "A Montenegrin soldier is talking to an Austrian soldier along the old frontier that formerly divided them. The Austrian asks: 'Why do you Montenegrins always go to war?' The Montenegrin replies: 'We are a poor people. We must plunder. Why do you go to war so much?' The Austrian answers, 'For glory and honor.' The Montenegrin says, 'Everyone fights for what he does not have.' Stalin guffawed."[6]

Djilas continued to recite a rollcall of local bloodshed. In one single battle during World War II forty partisans were slaughtered by Četniks in his native village. Milovan began to reflect on his rebellious countrymen: "They have the characteristics of primitive people. They are rebellious by emotion rather than by rational concept. Their psychology remains influenced by vestigial tribalism." His uncle Mirko had told him on his deathbed: "Remember, it is your sacred duty to avenge me." Djilas reflected: "Vengeance—this is a breath of life one shares from the cradle with one's fellow clansmen."[7]

At the age of nine Milovan was sent to secondary school in Kolašin. He amazed his cousin, a pro-Serb teacher and Democrat, by announcing he was a Communist, a claim as provocative as it was premature. He finished his secondary schooling at another institution in Berane.

In 1929 King Alexander of Yugoslavia, by then containing Montenegro, assumed dictatorial power and suspended the constitution. Deprived of free speech, a large proportion of the student population expressed their discontent by flirting with or even joining the Communist party, which was hallowed not only for its Marxist oppositional teachings but for representing Russian doctrine. Milovan openly proclaimed his Marxist affiliation while still in secondary school. He wore a shirt designed to imitate that of a Tolstoyan peasant and flaunted a bright red necktie. He resolved to go to Belgrade University, which was renowned as a hotbed of anti-regime sentiment.

According to Milovan anyone who managed to get to Belgrade then was entitled to University admission if he had a certificate of graduation from high school. He was excited to travel to the capital; it was the very first time he had ever seen a train.

Djilas' activism against those he considered his enemies became manifest during his university days. As he said to me once, "I think I am a typical Montenegrin in the sense that I am a product of that violent race." I observed that sociologically his life had been remarkable, spanning in one brief period the bridge between a vestigial feudal clan society in his childhood, then Marxist communism, heretical Titoism, and the withering away of Communism during a nuclear-missile age.

To this he replied, "I think my life has not been anything unusual. I always chose my own way. I never felt that I was doing anything extraordinary. I do what I must do in keeping with my beliefs, with my opinions, with my status as a man."

The "status as a man" of a Montenegrin, however, exceeded in rigors what it might be among tamer peoples. As he wrote in *Land Without Justice*:

So it has always been here: one fights to achieve sacred dreams, and plunders and lays waste along the way—to live in misery, in pain and death, but in one's thoughts to travel far. The naked and hungry mountaineers could not keep from looting their neighbors, while yearning and dying for ancient glories. Here war was survival, a way of life and death in battle the loveliest dream and highest duty.[8]

In 1912, when he was a year old, his father went off to fight in the First Balkan War. A year later he led skirmishes in the Second Balkan War. In 1914, when Milovan was three, his father had left home to fight the Austrians in World War I. When he was seven, Montenegro vanished into the union with Serbs, Croats, and Slovenes that became Yugoslavia, an idea the mountaineers had cherished for years but resented when it occurred. Many years later this chronology caused Milovan to wonder: "Are men doomed to become the slaves of the times in which they live, even when, after irrepressible and tireless effort, they have climbed so high as to become masters of those times?"[9]

Terrible brutality haunted his childhood dreams. "Everywhere on the roads wherever we went, there was sorrow—tombstones and graves, slaughter and misfortune. The murder of enemies was forgotten, but our own Montenegrin losses, especially if caused by a brother's hand, remained fresh in the memory . . . ."[10]

By the time of the Austrian invasion of 1914 and eventual occupation the little boy's soul was terribly scarred: "First they hanged three Montenegrins on a bare hill overlooking Kolašin . . . The black shadows on the high gallows lay across every soul throughout Montenegro."[11]

The unification with Serbia stimulated civil warfare. The rebellious Rovči clan was crushed and the insurgents "were treated with cruelty and insult. Their houses were burned down; they were pillaged and beaten. The women had cats sewn in their skirts and the cats were beaten with rods. The soldiers mounted the backs of old men and forced them to carry them across the stream. . . ."[12]

The ghastly turmoil that ravaged Montenegro between foreign and civil conflicts fostered the anarchic tradition of *hajduks*, the Robin Hood-type outlaws who had roamed the crags and forests since time immemorial. One of them, a political rather than social rebel, named Todor Dolović, was connected by marriage with the Djilas family and was respected and aided by Nikola, Milovan's father, who nevertheless would not permit his children to have any contact with even a respectable outlaw. Milovan says mildly: "He was not brutal. He was betrayed to the gendarmes by a peasant. They killed him in his sleep."

It is not to be wondered at that Milovan was not the best behaved lad. He reminisces: "I was not a good boy. My fantasy wandered. I rebelled very early against the society I found in Montenegro."[13]

Djilas finished his secondary school at Berane in 1929 and set off on his first great adventure that summer for Belgrade University. His father escorted him from his village to the small town of Kolašin. The two were on horseback, leaving home in the late afternoon because of a heat wave, travelling through the dark forest under "icy white moonlight." His mother had packed his belongings: a tin cup filled with cheese, a sweater, woolen socks.

At Kolašin he boarded a bus for Cetinje and there the first striking surprise greeted him—the train for Belgrade, a symbol of the burst from a peasant Montenegrin past to an active national and international future, about which he later wrote: "When a Montenegrin rebel meets Marxism-Leninism, the recognition is instantaneous and satisfying."[14]

With all the eagerness of a young man on the threshold of adventure he had determined he would eventually go to Paris or Prague to study journalism, although his father had suggested medicine. Instead, he enrolled as a student in literature. At the time of his arrival at the main intellectual center of his country the university was caught up in a wave of bohemian life: alcohol, tobacco, women; those who took their studies seriously were scoffed at.

By 1932 when he was first arrested by the political police, he had joined the Communist party and had become a party organizer. As a result he was imprisoned for three years and, in testimonial to his vigorous proselytizing among undergraduates, became a member of the Central Committee in 1938. By 1940, not yet thirty years old, he was a member of the Politburo and an associate of Tito.

Belgrade University was a demonstrable incubator of Marxist dogma and activist techniques. Milovan had shown revolutionary tendencies before he arrived at the somewhat sullen portals of higher learning; but it was there that he became an undergraduate in Communism. Before the outbreak of World War II he was to show himself an assiduous practitioner.

NOTES

1. Njegoš, Prince Petar Petrović. *The Mountain Wreath*. Translated by James W. Wiles. London: George Allen and Unwin, 1930.

2. Conversation with the Author, September 1984.

3. Conversation with the Author.

4. Ibid.

5. Ibid.

6. Ibid.

7. Ibid.

8. *Land Without Justice.* Op. cit., p. 39.

9. Ibid.

10. Ibid.

11. Ibid., p. 63.

12. Ibid.

13. Clissold, Stephen. *Djilas, the Progress of a Revolutionary.* Middlesex: Maurice Temple Smith, 1983.

14. Ibid., p. 12.

10

Communist

Starting in 1932 while still a university student and then continuing during his first of many terms in prison, Djilas worked as an illegal revolutionary stringently opposing the rightwing monarchy. He was jailed as a Communist in 1935 and, in 1936, entered a period of "intense illegality" until the Axis attack on Yugoslavia during the spring of 1941. He safeguarded his illegality by operating under false documents, travelling as the party's Central Committee ordered between Belgrade, Zagreb, and Ljubljana.

The papers obtained for him by the party required only a change in his photograph on journalistic documents he was given (as mentioned earlier) in the name of Deon Lapčević, a reporter for the newspaper *Politika*. He recalls with amusement that because of the prestige of "his" paper he was respectfully treated by policemen and other authorities and "I was regarded as a very important person; I paid only twenty-five percent of the price for railway tickets. All I had to do was show my journalist's card and I travelled very, very cheaply."[1]

Djilas proved himself a crafty clandestine agent and a skillful organizer. Despite his youth he was soon recognized in the underground Party's ranks as one of the leading agents, as he wandered about the country as "Deon Lapčević." The first time he met Tito was in 1937 after being sent by the party organization to Zagreb, the Croatian capital. Tito was not yet head of the party, which had its headquarters in Paris. From France the future Yugoslav boss organized an underground railway to dispatch recruits and supplies to the Republican side in Spain's Civil War. The party chief was named

Josip Čizinski, alias Milan Gorkić. In the late summer he was ordered to Moscow by Stalin and executed during the Great Purge. Tito posthumously rehabilitated Gorkić in 1977.

In response to orders from the Kremlin's dummy organization, the Comintern (Communist International), Tito was accepted, after his secret 1937 trip to Yugoslavia, as top man charged with reorganizing the illegal party and ensuring its loyalty to Stalin. When Djilas first saw him, Tito was the underground party's Organizational Secretary.

Tito came to Zagreb under one of his many false aliases—"Walther"—but, to his surprise, the young Montenegrin recognized him. "I had a memory of something," he recalls. "I told him, 'I know your name. Broz.'" When Tito inquired how he knew, Djilas told him of the portrait painted by Pijade while he and Tito were prisoners in Sremska Mitrovica earlier, and which Pijade had shown to Djilas. Milovan then said to him: "This means nothing. But you must know that if something happens, for example, if somebody tells the police, if I am arrested, you must know that I know your name. I will not tell them. If I tell, you must know that I was not a true comrade." Tito replied, "Listen, it doesn't matter."[2]

Djilas has a vivid recollection of Tito in 1937: "Already fat. Energetic, not long on explanations. He didn't like lengthy discussions. I liked his line and I was already inclined to dislike Gorkić who opposed an illegal organization and wanted only legal activity. But this was impossible in Yugoslavia. Tito was strong for an illegal party but at the same time favored such legal activities as we were able to manage. His views prevailed. He was an authoritarian."[3]

The two met in the apartment of a musician named Markola. "Tito was wearing ordinary clothes. He was a good dresser, as he always was," says Djilas. "The next time I saw him was later that year when we met in the Slovenian mountains. I went there together with my friend Lola Ribar."[4] (Ribar, an attractive, bright young man of good family, was killed by a German aerial bomb in 1943. He was about to fly off with Tito's first mission to the Allies, which he headed as a Politburo member. He had much abililty. I knew him before the war. His liberal father, not a Communist, was elected first president of Partisan-held Yugoslavia but was never more than a figurehead.)

In his pre-war meetings with Politburo members of the Yugoslav party Tito urged early starts to organizing and training the nucleus of an eventual military force. Djilas recalls being impressed that a group of sympathizers was developed within the Royal Yugoslav Army's officer corps. A youth organization was created and furnished with small arms thanks to friends in the regular army.

When Tito, a Croat, was placed in charge of the Yugoslav party, he named as his top associates in the underground Politburo: Edvard Kardelj, a Slovene; Aleksander Ranković, a Serb; and Djilas, a Montenegrin. This group functioned at the pinnacle of resistance during the war and well into the 1950s when first Djilas and later Ranković got into trouble with Tito and were ousted from authority.

The outbreak of World War II in 1939 had no immediate effect in Yugoslavia, although the royal government was frightened by the combined threat of Germany (since absorbing Austria, a menace immediately on the Northern frontier) and Italy, which was beginning to move toward the Axis orbit. This mute tendency was encouraged both by rightwing politicians and those on the far left who took a favorable view of the Hitler-Stalin pact of 1939.

On March 27, 1941, Tito came surreptitiously to Belgrade, some three months before Hitler broke his tryst with Stalin and invaded the Soviet Union. There was an almost immediate dramatic development in Yugoslavia when a British-sponsored coup d'état ousted the royal government, including Prince Paul, the regent. This produced a makeshift, officer-dominated regime that was clearly hostile to the Nazi-Fascist neighbors leaning eagerly over the borders.

On April 6, 1941, Hitler struck. Yugoslavia was wiped out, shattered and occupied by German and Italian troops after being divided into reconstituted "independent" political segments. Nazi bombers wrecked Belgrade, where Djilas was trying to organize a pro-Soviet demonstration. He stayed in the capital to arrange underground arms caches. The Communists who were to lead Tito's famous Partisan resistance remained immobile, awaiting developments. These came soon after Hitler's Russian invasion began on June 22, 1941.

That same afternoon Tito's Central Committee met. It issued an underground manifesto saying: "A fateful hour has struck . . . This is also our struggle." On June 27 the Central Committee established a headquarters of "National Liberation Partisan Detachments." Four days later Moscow wired requesting Tito to "start a Partisan War behind the enemy's lines."

Tito's die was cast on the morning of July 4, 1941. He met with Djilas and other members of the small Politburo in the villa of Vladislav Ribnikar, a prosperous liberal whose family owned the principal Yugoslav newspaper, *Politika*. Only five leading Communists, including Djilas, were present at this vitally important meeting.

For Djilas, the main result of the meeting, which signaled the beginning of the liberation struggle, was Tito's instruction for him to organize and command the projected conflict in Montenegro. He was both proud and happy. He reminisces: "I could think of nothing I wished to do more than go to Montenegro where, from time immemorial, ideas found consumption in sheer violence."[5]

As Djilas recalls those days, the Croatian fascist Ustaši had started massacring Serbs in Slavonia and other border areas between a new Nazi puppet state, Croatia and occupied Serbia. As the killings spread, an extensive, spontaneous rebellion started among the Serbs. All this happened during the spring prior to Hitler's invasion of the Soviet Union. Only on July 4, 1941, was an official decision taken by the Communist hierarchy to launch a unified, armed military struggle.

Tito's initial instruction to Djilas was to avoid any general uprising against the Italian occupation forces when he arrived in Montenegro. The mountain state's control had been assigned to Mussolini by the Fuehrer. Tito said: "The Italians are still organized and strong and they will break you," if he launched a precipitous attack. "You should begin with small operations. But shoot anyone—even members of the provincial leadership—if there is any sign of wavering or lack of discipline."[6]

With these stern instructions in mind, Djilas and his brother Aleksa left Belgrade July 5, 1941, and, travelling via Sarajevo, took a train to a suburb of Podgorica, a highland stronghold. He met with clan leaders to discuss the distribution of arms and ammunition already stashed away by the defeated Yugoslav army at the time of its surrender in April.

Milovan now recalls that the first effective Montenegrin uprising started July 13, 1941. This was directed by a staff he selected from the Montenegrin Communist Party. He actually led the assault but depended heavily on Arso Jovanović, subsequently partisan chief of staff, who had some military experience from service as an officer in the regular Yugoslav army. Jovanović supervised plans for the initial Montenegrin revolt.

After the first attack Djilas was astonished to find he could not limit the preliminary effort to small groups for minor incidents as Tito had proposesd. The restricted units formed under Jovanović's planning immediately grew into a spontaneous mass movement.

The story of Tito's remarkable creation of the Partisan Army, the most effective guerrilla resistance movement of World War II, is well known. Tito, as a brilliant commander and farsighted political leader, is a familiar to any 20th century historiography.

Djilas, as it turned out, was the only member of the small circle of Tito's intimates who had both a gift for guerrilla warfare (plus the temperament to enhance this gift) and also the eagerness for intellectual acquirements and avidity for political considerations. He showed great skill in using these attributes of crucial but informal warfare, without benefit of training. Finally, once poor Lola Ribar died, Djilas was the youngest immediate member of Tito's staff.

Much as Milovan admired Tito in those days, he venerated Stalin and was emotionally bewildered by the first hints of discord that greeted Yugoslavia's admission to communism's monolithic world. He was appalled at Stalin and aghast at the effrontery of Tito when the latter protested to the Comintern after it raised to embassy status the Moscow legation of the emigré Royal Yugoslav government (direct adversary of the Partisans). On August 3, 1942, Tito wired Moscow in a rage:

Can nothing be done to better inform the Soviet government of the traitorous role of the Yugoslav government and of the superhuman sufferings and hardships of our people, who are fighting against the invaders . . . Don't you believe what we are telling you daily? [The elevation of the exile representation to an embassy, higher than the mere legation status of Tito's mission] can have terrible consequences for our struggle. We emphasize the Yugoslav government is collaborating openly with the Italians and covertly with the Germans. That government is a traitor to our people and to the Soviet Union.[7]

The cynical tergiversations of Soviet policy remained incomprehensible and became increasingly outrageous to the Kremlin's faithful Yugoslav adherents, above all inexperienced youths like Djilas.

In mid–May 1943 the offensive, called Operation Black (*Schwarz*) by the Germans, was opened in the Tara valley area, a borderland country where Montenegro, Herzegovina, and Bosnia come together. This was an especially tense time for the Partisans. On May 15 Moscow dissolved the Comintern, which had previously served as Tito's conduit with Stalin. On May 11 the exiled Royal Government in London had uselessly ordered Mihailović to cease collaborating with Yugoslavia's Axis invaders and to arrange cooperation with the Partisans. And on May 15 the United States decided to send a mission to the very same Četnik forces that Britain had just abandoned in favor of Tito.

The principal series of battles that spring and summer of 1943 took place in the mountainous country around the rugged Durmitor massif. German, Italian, and Četnik units joined in an effort to trap and crush the main Partisan force. A parachute mission of British liaison officers and men, commanded by the diminutive but resolute Captain Bill Deakin, was dropped near Tito's headquarters during a tough period of fighting.

Deakin, a brilliant Oxonian who had served Churchill as a personal secretary and research assistant, soon met Djilas and was much impressed. In his splendid book *The Embattled Mountain*, Deakin recounts:

My first clear impression of him was during the last hours of the battle in one of the Bosnian villages north of the encircling ring, which had just been breached by Tito's forces. Milovan Djilas was endowed with the outstanding physical courage of the Montenegrin clans. . . . Saturnine and darkly handsome, he seemed to embody the legends of his divided land. This was the single impression first borne upon us. . . . By character intransigent, arrogant in the superficial certainties of Marxism as simplified in a student world . . . his nature was both complex and simple; rigid political beliefs of urban intellectuals had been imposed by a deliberate effort of will on the realism and honesty of a clansman. The tragedy of Djilas was to emerge long after the events at hand; the irreconcilable conflict between a rigid pitiless doctrinaire and the reflective imaginative artist of a mountain community of epic traditions.[8]

Djilas' rearguard battle was costly in lives and suffering and the Germans could boast of a battlefield triumph against the main body of Partisan troops, but Tito's forces won an important strategic victory by breaking out of Axis encirclement with about half of their total manpower intact. They marched through the river Piva's huge canyon while Djilas covered them with his small rearguard, about a third of whose number were already hors de combat with typhus.

The rearguard was heavily bombed by the Luftwaffe, but Djilas kept his troops divided into small units and hid the sick and wounded among rocks above the road along which they were escaping. As the Djilas command fought its way back toward the main army, it left a litter of wounded and sick casualities in rock caves. Some of these pleaded to be shot rather than risk Nazi capture. The Germans used police dogs to sniff out their hiding places. All survivors were murdered while Djilas' active force of about 1,500 fought its way westward to join Tito. The Germans ultimately closed the circle but the heavily smashed rearguard finally made contact with Tito's main army, which had successfully escaped annihilation. Djilas had allowed the execution en route of all Četnik troops, German Gestapo, and known political enemies as they were rounded up in pockets.

In early March 1944 Tito decided to send a military mission to Moscow. Djilas, as the best Russian linguist in the Politburo except for Tito himself (a Russian prisoner in World War I), was selected as the most suited from the high command to present its views to Stalin. The first Soviet mission under General Korneyev had been flown into Tito's headquarters one month earlier.

Djilas was overwhelmed with pride at being chosen for the return mission and being made its effective chief although the leadership was technically shared with General Velimir Terzić, acting chief of Tito's Supreme Staff. Tito took pains to instruct Djilas on how to answer any inquiries from the Soviets concerning a recent secret Partisan negotiation with the Germans on exchange of prisoners.

The mission was taken out by a small British plane which landed them in Bari whence they continued to Cairo, to Teheran, and thence by Soviet plane to Baku and Moscow. They arrived April 12, 1944. For more than a month Djilas and his colleagues were entertained and shown the sights as well as introduced to Soviet functionaries and representatives of other Communist parties, especially those from Bulgaria. The Yugoslavs were billeted in the comfortable Red Army Center, a hostel reserved for Soviet officers and ranking military visitors. Eventually there was a summons to the Kremlin where they were received by Stalin.

Djilas had already, before meeting him, written for the Yugoslav Communist paper *Borba*: "Stalin is the most complete man . . . He knows all and sees everything; nothing human is alien to him . . . There are no riddles in the world that Stalin cannot solve."[9]

Stalin was, of course, accustomed to such adulation, yet it is surprising that so independent a man as Djilas could have fawned to such a degree; a lapse he more than made up for in later publications, above all in his *Conversations with Stalin*.

During the Moscow stay of the Djilas mission, German parachutists made a daring attack on Tito's secret headquarters at Drvar, just failing to capture or kill the Partisan leader and his advisers. On June 5, more than a month after the first Kremlin visit by the Yugoslavs, and ten days after the audacious Nazi airborne assault against Partisan headquarters, Djilas received a surprise summons to Stalin's dacha. He was conducted by Molotov, Stalin's closest Politburo member. It soon became evident that this second summons had the purpose of warning Tito against the British. The Soviet leader said sarcastically:

During the first world war they were always tricking the Russians and the French. And Churchill. He's the kind of man who'll pick your pocket if you don't watch out. Yes, pick your pocket for a kopeck. Pick your pocket, by God, for a kopeck! And Roosevelt? Roosevelt's different. He dips in his hand only for bigger coins. But Churchill . . . ! Churchill will do it for a kopeck.[10]

A dispatch was brought in from Churchill announcing that Allied landings in France would begin the next day. Stalin commented sarcastically: "Yes, there'll be a landing—if there's no fog. So far they've always found excuses for putting it off. Tomorrow, I suspect, they'll find something else. Maybe they'll come across some Germans! Maybe there'll be no landing—just promises as usual."[11]

The Yugoslavs left Moscow several days later. They were taken to Tito's new, attack-free headquarters on the Adriatic island of Viš to which he had been evacuated by the British after the near-disaster of Drvar. Djilas was very much the man of the hour, the first Yugoslav to be received by Stalin. Apart from the Partisan leadership, his adored first wife Mitra Mitrović had been brought to the small island stronghold.

The Western Allies were pressuring Tito to form a coalition government under the pathetic little emigré King Peter. Tito was to serve as Minister of War. Conversations between the British and Yugoslav royalists on the one hand and Tito's leadership on the other provided a meaningless basis for hope.

In August Tito was flown to Italy for meetings with the Allied Mediterranean commanders and with Churchill. From these talks Tito obtained a compromise settlement for a three-man Regency until the question of King Peter's return was resolved. (This never came about.)

At the end of September 1944 Partisan units accompanied by a sizable Soviet force opened an assault on the Germans in Belgrade. Three weeks later Tito had entered the capital. Djilas was at Partisan headquarters in Croatia at the moment of Belgrade's liberation. Right after that he flew to Rome with Kardelj to meet the Italian Communist boss, Palmiro Togliatti, and discuss the possibility of settling the problem of Trieste, claimed by both the Italians and the Yugoslavs. The question remained unanswered then. On October 22 he and Kardelj flew to Valjevo, in Serbia, and drove by jeep on to Belgrade.

Although Milovan was at first widely regarded and feared in Belgrade as a stern, harsh Communist dogmatist, immediately after his arrival he began to alter his glowing views of Stalin's proud Red Army. General Zhdanov, the Soviet operational commander, ignored Yugoslav plans or intentions as the Belgrade offensive wound up; he was deliberately rude to Djilas. At the same time the latter began to hear the first sounds of a mounting roar of complaints against Soviet soldiers from the newly liberated peasants. The men who should have been greeted as friends and saviors misbehaved in the most outrageous fashion: looting, raping, robbing, and even holding up Partisan officers to steal their watches and revolvers. Today, more than forty years later, Djilas gets a stony look in his eyes when he recalls:

My conflict with the Russians first broke out in me that October. They raped our women and plundered our country as they occupied it. Tito called in the Soviet general who represented them, General Korneyev, to tell him that he, Tito, was discontented with the Soviet army and its attitude. He cautioned him in the presence of the rest of us, Kardelj, Ranković and me.

Tito told Korneyev that he was unhappy with Soviet military behavior. He spoke carefully, very diplomatically, and said this misbehavior was provoking a problem with our people.[12]

Only vague doubts about the future course of relations with Moscow as yet stirred in Djilas' mind. A plan had been considered by Tito and also by the new Communist leadership of neighboring Albania for the two countries to federate inside one republic, with Albania being joined to the very large Albanian minority in the Kosovo-Metohia special autonomous region of Yugoslavia that bordered both Macedonia and independent Albania.

But Stalin had played a tricky game when discussing this with the Djilas mission to Moscow and seemed to be urging Tito to take rash steps for no apparently valid reason. He also deliberately sought to foment trouble between Bulgaria, the most faithful Soviet satellite, and Yugoslavia. Uneasy stirrings crossed the minds of Tito and his associates.

Tito and his principal advisers were as one in the problem created by new shadows on the Soviet relationship. Djilas felt at home with his comrades in recognizing blemishes on the surface of relations with Moscow. These had started in an emotional and mass sense by the resentment and disappointment of the Yugoslavs. They were offended and infuriated by the behavior of Soviet troops. The worries of the political leadership were further disturbed by Moscow's apparent efforts to muddy the waters as far as Albania and Bulgaria were concerned.

Only later did Djilas resentfully conclude that "the peremptory, authoritarian characteristics of Yugoslav Communism . . . were essentially no different from those of Soviet Communism." On the contrary, he and the other Central Committee leaders loyally gathered into a solid phalanx around Tito during this initial time of troubles.

In March 1945, months after Djilas' tiff with General Korneyev in Belgrade, Milovan returned to Moscow for further talks with Stalin in a mission headed by Tito himself. Djilas and the others, including the London emigré Dr. Šubašić, designated as foreign minister in a government of "collaboration" the Western Allies were trying to produce, went to a hotel. Tito, as a mission chief and designated nominee for Prime Minister, in the coalition, stayed in the official Soviet guest house. In the sleazy old Metropole Hotel, a leftover from Czarist days, to his horror the puritanical Djilas was solicited on the telephone by a seductive female voice, a regular tarnished trick of the Soviet Security Police.

The purpose of this trip was to sign a Belgrade–Moscow Treaty of Friendship. At the customary dinner April 11, 1945, celebrating Kremlin signature of this document, Stalin challenged Djilas to drink a vodka toast to the Red Army. After his guest had done so, Stalin asked him directly what had been the difficulty between him and General Korneyev.

Djilas explained he had not desired to belittle the Red Army but to point out occasional instances of misconduct by some of its ranks. Stalin tried to laugh the explanation off, saying: "The Red Army is not perfect. The important thing is that it fights Germans—and is fighting them well. The rest doesn't matter."

Subsequently Stalin engaged in sneers at Djilas and even at Tito's high command. The atmosphere had not improved. And the idea of a collaboration regime with Tito serving as a kind of umpire rapidly vanished along with other Western dreams of rescuing East Europe from the cynical reality of Soviet military conquest.

In 1948 the split between the Communist allies became public knowledge as Yugoslavia was expelled from the Cominform, Moscow's new satellite "club," replacing the shades of the late Comintern. Yugoslavia also was dropped from the skein of Soviet alliances in East Europe. The startled outer world was at first skeptical as it saw torn apart the monolithic pattern to which it had become accustomed, if resentful. A torrent of abusive criticism of Tito, directed by the Kremlin, issued from all the satellite capitals. Hostile military maneuvers began to rumble on the Yugoslav borders. Belgrade responded by closing off its own frontier with Greece from any aid to a Communist insurrection there.

Djilas stood firmly by Tito in this astonishing quarrel. He openly allowed latent pro-Western feelings to emerge and even served as Tito's channel in a search for alliance with two NATO members, Greece and Turkey. In 1951 he had a conversation with Churchill, at that time no longer in his former Prime Minister's roost at 10 Downing Street. Churchill said to him: "You're a member of the Politburo, you've got a feeling for the Soviet mentality. If you belonged to the Soviet Politburo, would you invade Europe?" Milovan replied in the negative.

"But *I* would, you see," Churchill said. "What's Europe—disarmed, disunited? In two weeks the Russians would push right through to the English Channel. This island would defend itself one way or another, but Europe. . . . ? If it weren't for atomic weapons, the Russians might have made their move already."

Djilas countered that the Soviet Union was exhausted and had not yet recovered from the Nazi invasion, adding: "The fact that the Russians haven't invaded by now shows they don't intend to invade Europe." Churchill agreed: "They're held in check because Stalin is smart enough to shun adventures. And old—he's got no stomach for running around Siberia dodging atom bombs."

The conversation ended on a strange note. In what Djilas was to term "an almost compassionate plea," the old warlord begged: "Don't be too hard on the peasants—they're innocent, they're not to blame for anything."[13]

A cautionary suggestion from a wealthy English duke's grandson to the grandson of poor Montenegrin peasants!

Later that same year, 1951, General "Lightning Joe" Collins, U.S. Army Chief of Staff, visited Yugoslavia to discuss provision of arms. Djilas represented his government at a dinner given Collins by the U.S. ambassador. Urged to pass on a request by the top Yugoslav generals, Djilas asked for jet aircraft. The American general said it was not his sole responsibility and the United States had to give priority to demands from its Allies. Djilas reacted indignantly: "The one reason we can see is your ideological prejudice—we are Communists." Later on, he proudly recalls, the planes were supplied.[14]

I cite the above incident as indicative of Djilas' fundamental loyalty to his instincts, his friends and the ideas for which he had been enthusiastic. He was clearly suspicious of American policy at a time when Yugoslavia was seeking to realign its international position and build up its own defenses.

Likewise, his mistrust of and dislike for Stalin took a long time to manifest itself. And above all, it was a heartbreaking experience for him subsequently to break with Tito, the last survivor of Milovan's original gallery of those who could do no wrong. It is significant, I may add, that after each of these psychological shocks, once Djilas changed his mind it stayed changed: the early gods that had failed him remained "failed."

Within Yugoslavia Tito had established his uncompromising regime with implacable skill, avoiding even a remote appearance of cooperation with or recognition of the conservatives who had rallied around King Peter II, a feckless weakling. On May 15, 1945, the German army, still in Yugoslavia, had recognized the Partisan force as a "legal" Allied army and surrended to it. The last flicker of resistance came from Draža Mihailović and the remnant of his Serbian Četnik force. But the unhappy royalist, complaining that "the whirlwind of destiny" had been too strong for him, was trapped in 1946 by Ranković's OZNA, the secret police. He was hunted down, caught, tried, and executed.

The two great events in Djilas' life following World War II were his split with Stalin, which essentially meant a reflection of Stalin's split with Tito; and Djilas' own fight with Tito, which returned him in his older age to the role of his youth, a political oppositionist jailbird.

In a sense, Milovan, who is the most completely self-made and self-governed man I have known, became in himself the perfect free human of the 20th century although he spent so much of his life in prison for the sake of his changing ideas of freedom.

Milovan recalls the cases of two rightwing oppositionists: "Mihailović was given a death sentence and executed shortly thereafter. I heard that a high official in Security witnessed the execution, but I am not familiar with the details. In a minor sense, I am. He died well, as is to be expected of a Serbian officer." [15]

If Draža, the royalist and Četnik commander, was a symbol for Serbian nationalists who preferred a Greater Serbia to the concept of a federal Yugoslavia, the symbol of the Croats (second most numerous of the South Slav peoples) was Archbishop Alojz Stepinac. Djilas was party to discreet Communist negotiations with the Catholic clergy anent Stepinac, the Croatian primate. Milovan was admittedly startled when Tito once unconsciously used the phrase "I am a Catholic," which was technically correct in terms of his boyhood in a Croatian Catholic peasant household. When Tito indicated a desire to develop a "national Catholic Church" Stepinac, a loyal supporter of the Vatican hierarchy, displayed irritation.

It was Djilas who, at the Sixth Congress of the Yugoslav Communist party held in Zagreb, in 1952, drafted the Resolution that set a course toward liberalization in the form of a workers' self-management system to replace total nationalizations and agricultural collectivization. This was a step in the direction away from classic Communism and, indeed, the party's name was changed to "League of Communists," an early Karl Marx phrase. The Polit-

buro became the "Executive Committee" as the schism with So-
viet-type Marxism was underscored.

This trend toward original formulation of the dogma inherited
from Moscow continued in Djilas' mind. In 1954 he published a
series of startling pieces in the magazine *Nova Misao*, commencing
with a long essay called "The Beginning of the End and End of the
Beginning." This indicated that ideological ties with Moscow were
weakening and new trends were to be expected. As if an ideological
rupture with Soviet credo were not enough, that same year Milovan published an article in the official newspaper *Borba* attacking
and excoriating the social climbing, snobbery, and power-grabbing
habits of Yugoslavia's new, post-war, Titoist high society that governed all aspects of social life among the elite.

Djilas had been able to maneuver cleverly hitherto. He exploited
the split with Moscow to introduce a newly liberal trend among
the dogmatist elite, but his success was short-lived. Once he had
publicly criticized the wives of the "new class," they turned their
husbands wrathfully against the heretic. The original rift with Moscow now developed into a separate and internal rift with the party
leadership that had remained almost solidly behind Tito when he
broke with Stalin. It had not yet split off into another group of
malcontents irritated by a threat to its prerogatives and favored social and economic position.

Djilas was publicly attacked for acting "contrary to the opinions
of all other members of the Executive Committee." He requested a
meeting with Tito, which was also attended by Ranković and Kardelj. He was accused of "revisionism," a heinous sin in the Marxist
ledger. Tito called him "detached from present-day life" and saw
him becoming influenced increasingly by the Western political leaders he had met on journeys abroad. He saw Djilas as "a changed
man."

On January 16, 1954, a Central Committee session was convened
and its proceedings were broadcast by Belgrade Radio. Tito himself
opened the conference. He charged Djilas with arrogant behavior
and the assumption that he alone was right in his political views.
Tito insisted: "His case proves precisely how dangerous the class-
enemy in our country is."

NOTES

1. Conversation with the Author.
2. Ibid.
3. Ibid.
4. Ibid.
5. Ibid.
6. *Djilas, the Progress of a Revolutionary.* Op. cit.
7. Ibid.
8. Deakin, F. W. D. *The Embattled Mountain.* London: Oxford University Press, 1971, p. 129.
9. *Borba*, November 1943.
10. *Conversations with Stalin.* Op. cit.
11. Ibid.
12. Conversation with the Author.
13. Ibid.
14. Ibid.
15. Ibid.

11

Rebel

Djilas fought back. He argued in his speech: "From my boyhood until now I have been a free man and a Communist, and I hope to remain so until the end of my life."[1] But he was initially broken and confused. He announced on the second day of the proceedings that, in effect, he had changed his mind and would vote for the majority resolution condemning himself. Tito, not content with this victory over new ideas, closed the meeting by saying: "We shall . . . see how genuine his self-criticism has been."[2]

Djilas subsequently said: "Like the heretics of days gone by, like the sundry oppositionists in the Stalin trials, I proved my loyalty to the ideology and to the Party by recantation."[3] Nevertheless, on March 4, 1954, he enclosed his party membership card in a letter he sent to Communist Party Headquarters. He explained that, having resigned voluntarily from all the posts he held in the Communist League, he was now giving up his party membership.

On May 7, 1954, Tito told me he had "forgotten" Djilas. He added that Djilas had no influence and would never be permitted to rejoin the Communist League that he had voluntarily quit. It was obvious from the bleak look on his face that he now disliked Milovan personally.

Djilas was shattered. It took some time for him to recover his aplomb; he never lost his quiet resentment. The break left Milovan in a condition of emotional crisis and he told a visitor: "The face of my world was transfigured." This was no exaggeration. From being Vice President of Yugoslavia, he held no position, and he had no means of employing his time save by his own ingenuity and his determination to keep on writing. Almost every friend he had, ceased contact with him.

He was able to exist, financially, because he was not deprived of his pension, because there was still a market abroad for his books, and because his friend William Jovanovich, a Montenegrin–American publisher, arranged regular payments from his accumulated royalties. He was allowed to return to his comfortable but modest Belgrade flat on the street called Palmatičeva. For a man who was by nature gregarious, friendly, proud, and exceedingly active and eager to work, this was cruel isolation. Added to such punishment, he was forbidden (except in 1968[4]) to leave Yugoslavia until 1987.

The regime's retribution was not yet finished. The National Assembly, of which he was no longer a member, stripped Djilas of the parliamentary immunity granted deputies, and he was hauled up before a court in December 1954, charged with activities that would "damage abroad the most vital interests of our country" by "hostile and slanderous propaganda." This referred to his availability to members of the foreign press corps, eager for his opinions. The court sentenced Djilas to eighteen months imprisonment, the first since he had been jailed by the prewar monarch.

In his book, *Parts of a Lifetime*, Milovan recalls: "This society as a whole is obviously not yet ready for free discussion. I was silenced as an agent of the domestic and foreign bourgeoisie and spat upon as a petty-bourgeois devil—after twenty-two years of membership in the Party and over fifteen years within its highest leadership! . . . . I have a certain peace of mind, if also a certain bitterness."[5]

Years later, Djilas explained to me his own rationale along this tortuous road from orthodox Stalinist Communism to the new road of Titoism and finally his break with Tito's regime, for which he had fought so loyally and courageously. He analysed his reactions accordingly:

It happened in this way. After our conflict with Stalin I slowly developed in my mind different ideas, especially critical ideas of the Soviet Union. I compared this Soviet experience with our own and slowly I developed, point after point, critiques of the Soviet system and then of our own system which was not the same but had many similar traits. And I published my ideas.

I was overthrown from power in January 1954. They struck at me in every sense: in my private life, in the intellectual sphere, in every field. I was completely boycotted by my own comrades with whom I had worked during the prewar period, during the war and after the war. They struck at me in all ways. And I saw that Communism was producing an unjust society. I continued developing these ideas, but more radically.

One article that created a great stir was published in *Nova Misao* and this criticized the snobbery and climbing of the New Class. While I was being investigated, that *Nova Misao* article appeared and they used that as an excuse to say I was disloyal. Without that article I think there would have been less hatred and ugliness. But I was not content with what I had been seeing: plundered villas taken over by the new bureaucracy; stolen furniture.

The hierarchy started to get organized and I began to realize this was not some temporary weakness but much deeper. I remember thinking one day that capitalism had not resolved the problem of property and socialism had not resolved the problem of freedom.[6]

He clearly was angered by the lawless resolution of "property" that he saw with his own eyes in terms of pillaging by a new bureaucratic class at the expense of its predecessor. However, what he felt most urgently was the need for the revolution to "transform itself into democracy and Socialism . . . if it is not to be destroyed."[7]

He placed himself in an odd position by recanting some of his views and regretting his own behavior because, he reasoned: "I continued to feel that I was a Communist albeit hesitant about certain dogmas and felt like the heretics in the Stalin trials, who 'proved' their party loyalty by recantation."[8]

This was quite obviously a false line of reasoning because Djilas knew full well what was an open secret: that the victims of Stalin's great purges had been bullied and tortured into denying their actions, not persuaded by noble moral beliefs. He furthermore knew, as he later proved by his actions, that the errors occurring in postwar Yugoslavia represented the application and distortion of a proclaimed ideology to which he could obviously no longer adhere.

Tito bluntly denounced Djilas for a well-known Communist heresy: "Bernstein's heresy" (after the German Marxist, Eduard Bernstein, who insisted that the "primary goal of the workers' movement is the struggle for democracy"). Actually, there was no doubt some truth in Tito's observation, since Djilas, who denied Tito's charge, had evolved considerably from his earlier and fanatical revolutionary creed and was searching for democratic freedoms.

He remained in Sremska Mitrovica prison from December 1956 to January 1961. When he was granted conditional freedom he promptly got into trouble again and was returned for five more years until the end of 1966. His status as a state prisoner was held violated by the publication in America and Europe of *The New Class*, and his "conditional liberty" was seen as violated by the preparation of *Conversations With Stalin* shortly after his "conditional liberty" was granted.

In 1961 Djilas arranged with his publisher, Jovanovich, to deliver copies of the galley proofs (of *Conversations*) to me to use before publication in my newspaper column. Yugoslavia was then quietly seeking to improve its relations with post-Stalinist Moscow and Tito feared this move might jeopardize relations with the new Kremlin bosses. So Djilas was charged with revealing state secrets in this book and sent back to penitentiary for five additional years.

Both in the months between his trial and ultimate imprisonment in 1961 and during the period after his release Milovan was isolated from all but a tiny, brave handful of former friends and colleagues. When he and Stefica (the nickname of his second wife) went to the theater or a restaurant, virtually none of those he had known so well gave even the faintest indication they had seen him. The name of a street honoring his revolutionary deeds, Djilasova, was changed.

Few people dared come to see him, except for foreign journalists. Diplomats ignored him for fear of offending the regime to which they were accredited. His son, Aleksa, was made to suffer for his father's "disgrace" by being bullied when he was doing his regular military service near the Austrian border. Aleksa finally left Yugoslavia, after completing his tour of soldiering, and now lives abroad as an avowed dissident.

In prison Milovan kept a diary that indicates the difficulty of his life there. January 30/31, 1958:

5:30 rising. (In the summer an hour later.) 6:30 emptying the chamber pot; 10:30 walk (an hour and a half; up to now the walk has been usually at 8:30 and lasted only an hour); 1:30—dinner; 3:30—an hour's walk; 7:00 supper; 9:00—bedtime, by regulation (the bell rings fifteen minutes before that). I now go to bed around suppertime because I am cold. I seldom take supper, and sometimes not even breakfast (chicory coffee). During the day I lie dressed underneath three blankets and read with gloves on my hands. During the winter I give some crumbs to the sparrows. They have already got to know me and they are waiting. I want to help them during these cold, snowy days. The weather remains cold. Every evening around six they turn on the heat for about fifteen minutes. Not much help in that except one can go to bed a little more comfortably.

Fog in the morning. But during the day, beautiful blue skies. Food—breakfast—always chicory coffee. Dinner—potatoes, beans, cabbage (in winter, sauerkraut—very good), rice. The food is thicker than a chowder. There is little fat or spices, but it is well cooked and clean. Meat: three times a week (Tuesday, Thursday, Sunday) cooked in with the food, in very small pieces.

In comparison with the prewar food here in Sremska Mitrovica Prison the fare is no worse today. There is no less bread; it is even somewhat tastier. Without the addition of lard, sugar and vitamins, the food would be insufficient. Packages: ten kilos a month. And the right to buy in the prison store food up to a value of 1,500 dinars (including 1.5 kilograms of lard and a maximum of 1.5 kilograms sugar).[9]

In October 1968, Milovan benefited from a momentary easing in his official isolation. He was allowed a passport to go to the United States where he served as a visiting fellow in Princeton University's Woodrow Wilson School of Public and International Affairs. While in America he delivered the manuscript of his *Unperfect Society* to Jovanovich for publication in 1969. Djilas was honored while at Princeton with the Freedom Award of Freedom House, which had previously been given to, among others, Winston Churchill and Pablo Casals.

Although at his trial some of Milovan's enemies viciously asked that he be sentenced to death, he escaped the vindictive mood that embraced the party even since Tito's own security apparatus locked up those suspected of favoring Stalin against Tito in 1948. The latter were incarcerated on barren Goli Otok Island. Several thousand inmates there were brutally treated, starved, beaten, and placed on the same level as prisoners in Stalin's own Gulag system. Djilas described this horror later: "Goli Otok was the darkest and most shameful fact in the history of Yugoslav Communism . . . It was unimaginable humiliation."[10]

Ranković, the security boss, was overthrown in 1966, charged with involvement in a conspiracy to overthrow Tito. Djilas, who had been one of the triumvirate of Politburo chiefs closest to Tito, told me after Ranković's fall that he believed "such a conspiracy existed. Ranković had put his own men from the secret police in responsible party and political places. He did this carefully. Such a plan simmered . . . to take power after Tito, as chief of the party and chief of state."[11]

Djilas never saw Ranković after his own downfall. Since the UDBA (secret police), ordinary police, security forces, and prisons were all under Ranković's supervision, it is clear he harbored no soft spot for his former Montenegrin comrade. In fact, although it was obviously at Tito's behest that Djilas was forced to live in seclusion, his mail and telephone bugged, his visitors reported, and his trips abroad prevented, it is unlikely that Ranković stirred in the least to try to aid Djilas. Djilas told me: "I am permitted to travel freely in Yugoslavia, but not to publish anything. I am allowed to publish abroad but not to go there. They say they are afraid I might criticize my country in another land."[12]

NOTES

1. *The Progress of a Revolutionary.* Op. cit.
2. Ibid.
3. Conversation with the Author.
4. In 1968 he was given a passport in order to accept an invitation from Princeton University's renowned Wilson School of International Studies. This was at a time when Czechoslovakia, under the liberalizing Dubcek regime, was overrun by Warsaw Pact armies at Soviet behest. Belgrade wished to appear democratic in Western eyes. The passport was confiscated in 1970.
5. *Parts of a Lifetime.* Op. cit., p. 241.
6. Conversation with the Author.
7. Ibid.
8. Ibid.
9. Djilas, Milovan. Unpublished diary (made available to the Author).
10. Conversation with the Author.
11. Ibid.
12. Ibid.

12

Families

Djilas has always been acutely aware of his origins: Montenegrin tribe of Župa, clan of Vojnovići (the "warriors"), family of Djilasi (the "leapers"). Župa was wrested from Turkish rule in the mid-19th century. At the same time the Djilasi became more eminent among the clansmen of Vojnovići, a proud clan claiming descent from a 14th century feudal duke.

Murder, assassination—all forms of bloodshed—were familiar among Milovan's immediate ancestors. His paternal great grandfather, his two grandfathers, his father, an uncle, a sister and two of his three brothers were killed violently although, as he contends, "all of them yearned to die peacefully in their beds beside their spouses."

His earliest ancestral memories were the tales of his *hajduk* uncle, Marko Djilas, who lived as an outlaw for twenty-six years and who drove his wife away because he claimed she "smelled." Thereafter he lived alone in a mountain cave and was known to everyone as the "Berserker."

Milovan's grandmother Novka survived terrible feudal quarrels to die at the age of ninety-three after helping rear three generations of children on her tales of robber barons and monstrous Turks. His grandfather Aleksa added to the gory epic by shooting a family enemy and, with a dagger, carving out pieces of his heart.

To end this particular blood feud the Montenegrin ruler drove out the Djilas family with threats of vengeance. They fled to temporary refuge in Balkan Turkey but returned with their knives and

guns to establish themselves once more on their native soil as rebellious shepherds.

The royal Montenegrin prince, in order to put an end to the Djilasi feuds, ordered Milovan's grandfather's family to produce a son
for the first officers' cadet school of the Montenegrin principality.
This was Nikola, Milovan's father, who was arrested on charges of
planning to murder a member of the princely family, and was
thereafter shackled in heavy irons for a year.

Nikola, a garrulous, quarrelsome man, swore an oath of allegiance to the Prince in exchange for dropping the charge of con-
spiring against the royal clan. The Prince appointed him to his border patrol and granted him land in Podbišće, still a restless hamlet.
Nikola built a sod house, which was eventually replaced by a two-
story stone dwelling on a bluff above the Tara river, Milovan's
childhood home.

The father was one of the first generation Montenegrin officers
with even a slight claim to any education. He gave his family an
austere life but for himself and his guests there was always coffee
and plum brandy. His life as a frontier guard was stern as he squashed
plots against the regime; suspects were whipped with wet ropes.
He led his local forces of young men "eager for war and blood and
greedy for glory."[1]

Milovan remembers his father well: riding a high and slender mare,
"himself slender in his gray uniform, all trim, in boots and with a
revolver in his belt" or later, "gray and gaunt, like a wolf which
runs and runs through the mountains." "That slimness and light-
ness made him handsomer and more tender toward us [children].
Father was sick with the love he bore his children."[2]

This dour man lived to the age of 73 when he was murdered by
Albanians in the village of Srbica for no other reason than that he
was a prominent Serbian Orthodox Montenegrin. Milovan still remembers him as "nimble like an old wolf," and "a tireless talker
with a boundless imagination."[3]

Despite the son's vivid memory of his fierce father, he acknowledges that his taciturn mother was the dominant parent in terms of
influence on the children. He recollects: "In the Montenegrin tradition she was a solemn, somewhat forbidding tall woman, always
garbed in black, her long face with lantern jaw wreathed in its black
scarf, her eyes mirroring solemnity."[4]

She never quarrelled with the villagers or her own in-laws. When she deemed it necessary to beat the children, she did so quietly, without cursing or scolding. "Her wisdom was simple, unobtrusive, but real and somehow instinctively infallible whenever it appeared."[5]

The mother of the family was not Montenegrin but came from a Serbian mountain clan called Radenovići-Merešanti in Plav. Milovan recalls: "Mother's kin differed in everything from the Montenegrins. They tilled the soil better. Their food was tastier and more varied. They dressed better and gave more importance to cleanliness . . . The Merešanti were a proud people but unostentatious . . . Mother, too, was different from the Montenegrin women. She was cleaner, more industrious, more domestic. She closely resembled her father and brothers—tall, big-boned and fair."[6]

This austere woman ran an efficient home. Milovan remembers:

Our household was completely peasant. The plates were not matched but there were plates. Also blankets and coverlets. Mother waged a determined but unsuccessful battle against lice and fleas, helped to flourish by the presence of the cattle in a manger on the ground floor. Although there were occasional hired hands, she always labored at least as hard as the other peasant women.

Nothing could surprise or frighten her very much. She mourned simply and deeply, without many words or much outcry. She rejoiced in the same way, unnoticeably, the way she breathed. She bore within herself certain immutable and strict rules of honesty, justice, truth, faithfulness, mercy, reliability. Though hardly visible and unproclaimed, these immutable laws burst forth in her instantly and with unusual vigor if anyone violated them.[7]

What a splendid tribute from a son to his mother!

Milovan recalls the brutal death of his father accordingly:

In October 1943 two Albanians came and killed my father without any investigation, without any reason. They took him out of the house and shot him. They came in the room of a small house where my parents lived in Srbica and simply took out their guns and shot him. They didn't ask him anything and they just stole his coat off a hanger on the wall and left. My mother was there. She managed to take my father in her arms and her hands were filled not only with blood but also parts of the heart and kidney, the insides.[8]

Milovan had two wives during his life and is proud of the fact he never had any mistresses, an unusual boast for a Montenegrin. He admits to carnal violations of this trust only a few, unsentimental times. As a boy he learned about sex from a hired hand, Kosa, a sturdy mountain girl with soft yellowish eyes, "good-natured, gay and tireless." He recalls: "I fell in love with the enticing warmth and softness of her body."[9]

He confides: "I am not a sinful man although I am not an angel. In my life I had a few temporary adventures that lasted a short time. But not while I was married."[10] His first great love was for a fellow student at Belgrade University, Mitra Mitrović, a year younger than himself but studying in the same faculty of Literature. He met her at a seminar in the Russian language.

Mitra came from a very poor Serbian family from Užicka Požega. Her father was a railway employee; her mother a hotel servant. She had three sisters and a brother and all of them were good scholars who completed high school.

Milovan met Mitra in 1932 but his courtship was interrupted by his first imprisonment a year later. He married her in 1933, formally, in a church. At that time civil marriage was not legally permitted in the Yugoslav province of Serbia. But Milovan wanted a legal wedding because under the law a wife had the right to send letters to and visit a husband held in prison.

Despite separation during penitentiary terms and the Partisan war of Tito, they remained married until 1948. They separated then and divorced in 1950, after Milovan had fallen in love with his second and present wife, Stefanija. Although Mitra was hurt and angry, she retained relations with Milovan. They had one daughter, Vukica (Serbian for "she-wolf"), born in 1948, who lives in Belgrade where she often visits her father and her stepmother with whom she is on good terms.

Milovan recalls his youthful love for Mitra. She was slender and pale with black hair and dark eyes. Her skin was white and she had long, delicate fingers. He was impressed with her shapely breasts visibly outlined beneath the sweaters she favored. He thought of her as "my woman." As he remembers:

Our love had a somewhat different beginning from the usual love affair between young Communists. It was love from the first instant. That is to say, I knew I was a Communist and she knew she wasn't and we fell in love not because we saw things alike ideologically, but because we couldn't keep away from each other.

At first I thought she found me attractive because of my reputation as a young writer. Other people, particularly women, thought so too. Having sensed that, she ignored, even underestimated, that side of me. At first I was angry, and then pleased—our relationship was developing unencumbered by any strains, uncomplicated and pure. But I was sorry she was not a revolutionary and a Communist.(Later Mitra became a Communist and she was a wartime Partisan).[11]

Years of separation by penitentiary bars and war perforce had their effect and Djilas, toward the end of the war, fell in love with a young blond Croatian girl. Three years after peace came he separated from Mitra. She remained politically loyal to her husband and she stood by him during his troubles with the Tito regime and his consequent disgrace and imprisonment. Today she and Milovan and Stefanija are friendly.

Mitra paid in suffering for Milovan's troubles, despite her divorce. Their daughter, Vukica, told me:

She suffered especially. I was a child and had only a few little incidents with children who had heard in their homes that my father was in jail. They would yell at me. When we were nine years old one boy shouted 'Your father is in jail' and I went home crying. My mother took me by the hand to his father, who opened the door, newspaper in his hand, and my mother explained the situation. He was very embarrassed.

Right after the Party Plenary session in 1954, when my father was denounced, mother was boycotted and all the people supposed to be her friends abandoned her. It took three or four years and after she was once seen shaking hands with President Tito things changed. She remained a member of Parliament even after the Plenary session [that denounced Djido].

She made a speech there they didn't know what to do with. She defended my father on political grounds but her defense was of a kind they couldn't just repeat. Yet because she defended him she was boycotted and suffered the consequences, although she even managed to get a job because the government realized she was not a threat. And in a subtle way, in a very tricky way, she even managed to defend him although she didn't share all his views. At first, to protect me from trouble, my mother listed my name in school and so forth as Vukica Mitrović. But I switched to my father's name when I finished primary school.[12]

Vukica now leads a normal life in Belgrade but she stays out of any organizations "because there might be trouble; because some people might try to please the government more than the government is asking to be pleased. I am trying to avoid the opportunity for being persecuted by officials or blocked in something I want to do."

Vukica has a matter of fact, realistic view of her father's second marriage. Speaking like a modern young woman anywhere in the Western world she says: "He fell out of love with her [Mitra]. They'd been together for quite a long time, being lovers as they could whenever they could, but that wasn't too much. And then after the war . . . I don't know if he changed a bit. You know how it goes. When people have been together. My mother's side of the story, as they say. It's just that he stopped loving her the way he used to love her when they were younger. He simply fell in love with another woman. I love my father although we are of different temperaments."[13] (And of course she is devoted to her mother.)

Djilas says today that the collapse of his first marriage was connected with his break with Leninism and the Yugoslav party bureaucracy and his turning to his first passion, literature. All this came about at a moment when he was greatly attracted to the pert young Croatian girl, Stefica (the Yugoslav nickname) Barić, to whom he is still wedded almost forty years later. This enduring love affair stemmed, says Milovan, from "intellectual as well as emotional reasons."

Milovan recalls that both Stefica and Aleksa, their young son, suffered from his position. "We understood this as if it was a war and we were sending our boy to the war," he remembers. In his book *Rise and Fall*, Milovan recalls that when he emerged from the Serbian Government building where the process against him was held in Belgrade, "Stefica was waiting for me . . . She saw me coming out pale and gray. I told her they would arrest me. On a walk that evening, I complained that I didn't feel like going back to prison, that I was still having problems with my nerves. She was consoling: 'Aleksa and I will come to see you; we'll take care of you. You'll survive this too.' "[14]

Two days later he was taken away by the police. He remembers gratefully: "The only living being to merge heart and soul with me was Stefanija." On January 20, 1961, when he was conditionally released from the penitentiary and departed with a stern lecture from the warden ringing in his ears, Stefica and Aleksa were waiting for him on a gloomy winter day.

Štefka, as Milovan usually calls her, first met Milovan in 1946. She was a lesser member of the Croatian party apparatus and a good Communist, who had held a dangerous job in Zagreb during the war, linking the secret underground with the Partisan army. She came from a petty bourgeois family of trades people and was just ten years younger than her husband. They were formally, officially, married in 1952, after an open liason of more than two years, and Aleksa was born in 1953. Aleksa was not yet four when his father was arrested by the Tito regime.

Milovan says of his boy: "He suffered very much. I think that until today some consequences still exist in his mind and his psychology, his sensitivity. He regularly visited me in prison with Stefanija. It was he who decided to go abroad and work as a dissident; I didn't participate in making up his mind, but I approved."[15]

Aleksa, who has been active in the Yugoslav political emigration, admits:

My boyhood was deeply affected by my father's political difficulties. I experienced both intensive sympathy and animosity because of him. The latter was primarily from party bureaucrats and their children.

My father did not spoil me. In any case when he finally came out of prison I was already thirteen years old. But he was not very strict with me either. I always felt very close to him.

When he was in prison for nine years I visited regularly [around 116 journeys to prison]. One interesting problem for my father was that he could not properly get my mental age. He would either overestimate it or underestimate it. When he was in prison and I was around ten years old he once began a rather serious discussion with me about Cervantes and (if I remember correctly) Rousseau's "Confessions." And although I was reading both at that time I could not follow his arguments. And then he would suddenly talk to me as if I were a child.

I believe that my father and mother had an unnaturally harmonious marriage exactly because she supported him so consistently during his prison years and otherwise. This created such a strong bond that minor disagreements could not upset it at all. In any case, such disagreements were rare.[16]

Aleksa concedes that being his father's son was disadvantageous to him in Yugoslavia. In London he says he has found abroad "a certain sympathy from the intellectuals in the West who are interested in Communist countries." Although he had had a hard time doing his Yugoslav military service "some officers behaved decently and some even showed benevolent interest."

Aleksa seems to have cool relations with his half-sister, Vukica, but with her mother, Mitra, "My relations are very friendly. I find her interesting and good company. I think she likes me but I cannot claim that we are very close. Yet considering that we are not relatives our relationship is excellent."[17]

If one assesses the tragedies, strains, and disadvantages occasioned by Milovan's political difficulties, wartime, and prison absences, one may only say that he has been a lucky husband and a good father to his children, both of whom love and respect him greatly.[18]

NOTES

1. *Parts of a Lifetime.* Op. cit., p. 36.
2. *Land Without Justice.* Op. cit., p. 18.
3. *Parts of a Lifetime.* Op. cit., pp. 36, 37.
4. *Land Without Justice.* Op. cit., p. 18.
5. Ibid.
6. Ibid., pp. 27, 28, 36.
7. Conversation with the Author.
8. Conversation with the Author, Podbišće, September 1984.
9. Ibid.
10. Ibid.
11. Conversation with the Author.
12. Conversation with the Author, Belgrade, 1984.
13. Ibid.
14. *Rise and Fall.* Op. cit.
15. Conversation with the Author.
16. Letter to the Author from London, February 1985.
17. Ibid.
18. At this writing (1988) Aleksa had a fellowship at Harvard.

13

Ideologue

Milovan Djilas has earned a place among 20th century political thinkers by contributing a single but profoundly important theorem to the analysis of Marxism. Like the hedgehog in Sir Isaiah Berlin's famous analogy between that animal and the fox—the fox knows many things, the hedgehog knows one big thing (how to curl up and protect itself)—Djilas knew one big thing. He discerned a fundamental truth clearly and expressed it in lucid language that answered a question asked in countries of all ideologies: Why does Communism falter when its progenitors gain power and put its tenets to the test of practice?

At the time he voiced this heretical and destructive thought, Djilas was still a top member of the Communist hierarchy of Marshal Tito's Yugoslavia. His theory of the New Class elaborated in the late 1940s and early 1950s explains that in any Marxist revolution, the old governing class it removes politically, and also in an economic sense, must inevitably be replaced by a New Class. This then, when it takes power, deteriorates morally and, as Lord Acton said a hundred years ago, such power brings corruption with it. Djilas adds:

I think this is inevitable. I think that a classless society is impossible. This is utopian theory. The best society is a class society, in which the classes have the possibility to fight for their own aims, respecting the laws. This is not a new idea. It was really expressed in Machiavelli only he didn't speak about class, he spoke about different parties and so on. He meant the same thing in his own time, with his own knowledge which was different than ours.

The idea of class was introduced into revolutionary theory by the French revolution. But we may find some rules, some remarks by Machiavelli, not so explicitly expressed, and even by the Italian theoretician, Vico.

It seems to me that Marxist revolutions of the twentieth century—and they've all taken place in the twentieth century—for example Soviet Russia, North Korea, China, Vietnam, Poland, Czechoslovakia, Rumania, Albania—all of them have been infected by a class system which became deformed and to which I refer in my theory as the New Class.

You cannot achieve a revolution, a Marxist revolution in today's world without having the germ of a new class leading that revolution and then when the revolution succeeds the germ grows into a large creature and takes control of the society.

I must add that the beginning of New Class is the Leninist theory of "New Party" and in this theory of professional revolutionaries, when he discerned what was needed. It was after the first revolution in Russia in 1905–1906, when his party was dissolved, and he said that what was required was professional revolutionaries. This is the germ of "New Class."[1]

Djilas' great contribution to political theory was the axiom that in all Marxist revolutions, the old ruling class is eliminated and replaced by a new ruling class that swiftly assumes most if not all of the responsibilities of its predecessor and also some of its social attributes. It is then corroded morally by its success. Djilas adds:

I have seen this phenomenon in the Soviet Union and Yugoslavia. And I have studied the same pheonmenon in all Eastern European countries. Bulgaria, Hungary, in Poland, in Albania, all at first closely connected with Soviet influence.

I reluctantly came to conclude that it is absolutely inevitable and unavoidable that when there is a Marxist revolution which succeeds in any country, a subsequent factor must be and will be the application of these rules of the "New Class." In other words, a Marxist revolution is inevitably followed by a new group of rulers who establish a class dictatorship in the name of revolution.

Because the Communists insist theirs is a classless society, they transform themselves into a monopolistic class. And this is the process of how they start to be a ruling class. Then when they have done that, by controlling all means of information and propaganda, they announce that their society is classless. Now I think not many Communists in Eastern Europe believe it's classless. But they see that power is comfortable for the rulers and they have accommodated themselves opportunistically.

It is simply Lord Acton's law—power corrupts and absolute power corrupts absolutely.[2]

Djilas' New Class theory and the book by the same name struck a telling blow at Communism's effort to gain moral ascendancy in the 20th century world. He makes no predictions on how China's "real New Class" will succeed but, he adds, "This is better than Mao Zedong's Cultural Revolution and better than Stalin's period of cruel terror; it is better for society. And Gorbachev might modify the Soviet system; but his new aides all stem from the old New Class hierarchy."[3]

With his one acutely perceptive theory Djilas carved out a position as an important 20th century political theorist. He insists:

I am not a great socio-political philosopher. Practically everything I said was in part really said earlier by this author or that author. My enemies have said I was influenced by Eduard Bernstein, the German socialist who envisioned gaining power without violence. He did not influence me. Nobody really influenced me.

In this sense, this is an absolutely completely original work. But later, reading some books, I know for example that Bertrand Russell spoke in one of his works about how Communism is the creation of some new elite, some new class. But I didn't know this when I wrote my book. Of course, he didn't know this when I wrote my book. Of course, he didn't elaborate. The same point of view is given by the Russian religious philosopher Berjaev, one of the founders of personalism, personalistic philosophy. I found this out later in a lecture of Bukharin [Soviet Communist leader liquidated by Stalin]. In one lecture in about 1922, he said: "Comrades, if we continue this way we will be transformed into something like a new exploiting class." It is interesting that such opinions existed earlier although they were not developed in a complete theory. But I didn't know about them. When I elaborated my theory and wrote my book, I wasn't influenced by anybody; it was my own experience and my own thoughts alone.[4]

In 1985 I asked Milovan: "Does your theory of the New Class apply to all revolutions in which the authorities in power are overthrown and replaced by new revolutionary movements or only to Marxist revolutions because of their particular class aspect? For example, was there any hint of a 'New Class' in the French Revolution?"

MD: "I think the position of my book, *The New Class*, may be applied only to Marxist-Leninist revolutions. Not to the others. The fact is that in every revolution, you may find some tendencies, not the same but similar tendencies, toward transformation of the revolutionary body into some privileged social group later, when they take power. But only in Communism, with the nationalisation of means of production and with the totalitarian force of political life, was it possible to be transformed in some new ruling class or group."

CLS: "Is this because the elite which had been running industrial and state machinery was eliminated and had to be replaced and therefore a new class was required?"

MD: "This is so. Plus the fact that they also want power and take all means of information and all means of propaganda to maintain their position. You cannot separate these two. It means dictatorial power, monopoly of information and monopoly over industrial machinery, over means of production.

"But such forces you find only in Marxist-Leninist movements, very strongly influenced by Marxism-Leninism, which may be nationalistic. For example, Algeria. The program of the Algerian Front for National Liberation was consequently like Marxism-Leninism. It was strongly nationalistic but in every other way very similar to Marxism-Leninism. I think that some of those leaders during the revolution were powerfully influenced by Marxism-Leninism, like Ben Bella, for example.

"In the French Revolution at the end, after the revolutionary process finished, it was the bourgeoisie that was the principal actor in the revolution, including the *sans culottes*, lawyers, intellectuals, peasants, and so on. But they didn't nationalize the means of production, and did not take over a monopoly of information . . . ."

CLS: "They didn't necessarily require a class to run things?"

MD: "Yes, that is so."

CLS: "Do you think any other revolution in the past, prior to Marxism-Leninism, was marked by a deliberate desire to replace the old ruling class with a new class in order to keep the state going, or was it only a requirement that was brought in by the first successful Marxist-Leninist revolution, in the Soviet Union?"

MD: "We only find this phenomenon in Marxist-Leninist revolutions. Every revolution, even in the past, tends to be transformed into some form of dictatorship. The French revolution, as you know, was transformed into the Napoleonic dictatorship. The English 17th century revolution resulted in Cromwell. The only great revolution, *great* I mean, which was not transformed into a dictatorship was the American.

"And we know why not. Because Americans really have no poor class, like *sans culottes* or proletariat. Secondly, which I think is very important, is that Americans have not got such elaborate theories as those of Rousseau in France. They only have some religious differences which they tolerate between themselves and their revolution was founded in the spirit of tolerance."

CLS: "Can you think of any particular event, incident, or fact that you read about which started you thinking along the lines that became your New Class thinking? No single event or book or idea?"

MD: "No, I cannot. Nothing—but I may remember some events. For example, this conflict between Stalin and Yugoslavia. I tried to explain slowly to myself what the rules of such a conflict are, because we were almost completely innocent in this conflict. They really attacked us for purely hegemonistic reasons. And I said to myself, why is this possible in Communism? And later, when I saw that Yugoslavia would not take a democratic path, some way to a more just society, I also started to criticize Yugoslavia. Yugoslav officials, Yugoslav policy. And then when they persecuted me, they didn't permit me to defend my views after I was thrown out of the party . . . ."

CLS: "That was in 1954?"

MD: "Exactly. 1954/55. I saw that they really attacked me as an innocent. I mean innocent in a political sense. And they dared to liquidate me spiritually, not permitting me to publish any literary works."[5]

Like many political philosophers who have had an ideological influence in history, Milovan Djilas was born at a time of surging restlessness and change, both in the world and in his native Montenegro. During his childhood, youth, and early manhood this played an important role in the formation of his character and personality in somewhat the same way as the effect of the 18th century on the French *philosophes* or on the American patriot leaders in the quarrel with England that led to independence. The seething effects of the industrial age in Europe that encouraged Karl Marx to apply his formidable concentration and willpower to the elaboration of new systems and the techniques of producing them, and the upheaval of World War I that enabled Lenin to apply these ideas and techniques in Russia, slowly found their way to the Balkans.

When Djilas was a student, the giddy impact of Soviet communist ideas began to percolate among the South Slavs and by the time World War II hit them in 1941, he was already a leading member of Tito's astonishingly successful movement. When this turned against Stalin's menacing embrace, the young Montenegrin began to elaborate his special theory of the New Class. Djilas is quite aware that with particular respect to his political concepts he was a child of his time. He says:

I remember, when I was a very young boy, seven or eight or nine years old, close to my native village lived a peasant who felt himself a Communist. The peasants knew him as a Communist, and jokingly they spoke about him as "the Communist." And he was beaten by the police. This was the fact which attracted the peasants toward him, to joke with him, to gossip about him, to praise him. He was a very nice person, very sympathetic. He was not aggressive in any way. And this is interesting. He attracted me.

I saw in him some inclination toward justice, toward brotherhood and so on. Then when I was in the gymnasium, the upper school, in a nearby village, there was one student of medicine whom I met. I lived with my aunt who was his relative. When he came from Belgrade, he spoke to me about Communism. I was still young, about eleven or twelve only. And this also influenced me. I think that somebody is born a Communist, that means with some inclination to be Communist, and then later he learns the theory and ideology, which changes and corrects many of his idealistic inclinations.

I think through all my period of Communism, I was inclined to idealistic beliefs, but at the same time I learned to be a practical political man, a practical Communist. It's strange to tell you but, for example, I read the critique of a recent book of mine written by an English lady who reproached me that I had once been chief of "Agitprop" [Agitation and Propaganda] in our Party and she said that I was a liar when I was preaching lies.

This is not true, this is wrong. This is the wrong approach. Because in politics, what you believe *at the time*—this is the truth for you. Never mind what ideology—right, left, center, and so on. For me, I didn't know whether it was scientifically, exactly true. Now I know. But *this was for me the truth at the time*.

I changed with time from this idealistic approach that means believing in the *perfect* society, toward an appreciation of an *unperfect* society. Speaking about the "new class," I still now think many points of view are not correct from the scientific point of view, but I still believe now that it is the key to the understanding of Communist society.

Without knowing modern political theories, from my personal experiences I made a synthesis about Communism. In this way, I think I am original. In this way only. But it would be wrong to take me as a great person or thinker. I am none of these.

I think *The New Class* was really original, a completely original work, in the sense that I didn't know others with similar thoughts then when I wrote it. But later I elaborated somewhat. *The New Class* still is a Marxist book by method, by essential point of view. And this is a quality of the book, because when one reads it he feels that this is something exactly taken from experience, because this is still Marxist. Even now, in method of writing, I am rational and precise in composition. This is still Marxist. This discipline in method—in this I am still Marxist.

It's strange, with Communism. From the point of view of Communism, everything in practice is the opposite to theory. For example, Communists are against war. But now only Communist countries are warlike. For example, Communists are entirely against nationalism. And yet, in our time, they are among the world's worst nationalists. Take Albania or Vietnam or Bulgaria. Communism teaches equality, but Communist society is among the least equal societies in the world.[6]

Djilas demonstrated convincingly that an ultimate consequence of Marxism wherever it succeeds in taking over control is the inevitable creation of a new ruling class, corrupted by its own power. And (per Acton's doctrine), holding complete power in its own hands, the new class becomes completely corrupted. This is not a complicated doctrine to pursue. It is one big thing, in the world of political theory, much like Berlin's hedgehog. Djilas knows perhaps only one thing new in Marxist theory, but it is vast. It helps explain the inhumanity of Marxist successes and why in all such newly Marxist states the only true beneficiaries are those of the ruling class—now hereditary—just as had been the case under the previous systems.

The New Class assessed by Djilas is often, but not always, competent; but it is also almost always diverted from its proclaimed aims of governance for the people if not by them, as a result of its personal attraction to the trappings of authority—luxury, laziness, snobbism, bossiness, and pure outright theft.

In a human sense, Djilas proved his integrity by resigning from this new class as it were. He was one of the principal beneficiaries of power and the corrupt temptations of power presented to the New Class by the Yugoslav revolution. But he limited his corrupt benefits—above all by comparison with his fellow political chieftains. And he voluntarily gave up power and all that went with it by getting into a fervent argument with the other members of the Politburo.

He sacrificed all gain as a matter of principle, something that has been unknown in the entire Marxist world since it first took over Russia in 1917. Thus by personal integrity he was eligible to join Acton as a modern philosopher of resistance to an evil state.

NOTES

1. Conversation with Author, Bovec, Yugoslavia, July 1985.
2. Ibid.
3. Ibid.
4. Ibid.
5. Ibid.
6. Ibid.

14

L'Envoi

Josip Broz Tito, a son of Catholic Croatian peasants who tradition-
ally owed allegiance to a centralized Roman Catholic church and an
imperial source of foreign power, Vienna's Austro-Hungarian empire, was not a traditional rebel. His ideas were ignited as a Russian
prisoner of war in a moment of insurrection. As a revolutionary
leader he was brilliant; as a political philosopher he was midway
between Stalin's brutal dictatorship and Djilas' dream of freedom—
a decompression chamber of Marxism.

The Yugo or South Slavs are descended from a gifted, vigorous
race that had passed on to the great Slavonic world the Christian
culture of the Greek Saints Methodius and Cyril, including the
modified Grecian alphabet devised by the latter to present religious
scriptures in Cyrillic to converted Slavs. The northern Slovenes and
Croats ultimately came under the joint suzerainty of Vienna and
Rome with their Latin alphabet. But the Serbian peoples, who
dominated South Slavdom then and now, built up a splendid and
vibrant pre-Renaissance civilization that was stillborn after its destruction at Kosovo in 1389 by the Turkish armies of Sultan Mu-
rad.

That disaster put an end to the rich cultural development already
under way in feudal Serbia. It throttled the possibility of independent growth linked to Byzantine Constantinople. A sullen and hu-
miliated Serbia was unable to benefit from the inspiration of the
cream of the Byzantine Greek scholars and artists who, when their
great capital fell to the Turks in 1453, fled to Italy. The Renaissance
blossomed in Italian city states while unhappy Serbian-Montenegrin

peasants sorrowed under Moslem sovereignty. They sewed black bands of mourning for Kosovo around the rims of their traditional pillbox caps.

Until the 19th century this bondage remained. It is still deeply engraved on the memory of a vigorous and imaginative people. The Serbs always dreamed of freedom and fertilized similar reveries among their Croat and Slovene cousins. The latter were ruled by another imperial agglomeration, centered in Vienna. However, neither the Orthodox ex-subjects of the Ottoman Sultan nor the Catholic Slavic subjects of the Habsburg imperator managed to achieve a true modern freedom until the end of World War I, in 1918. Milovan Djilas, who typified the political dream of South Slavic liberty, was born just seven years earlier.

My favorite South Slav hero is Prince Marko, the Serbian king's son, who rode about the countryside on his horse Šarac, doing battle against the conquering *paynim*. And whenever they stopped to lunch in a village tavern, Marko generously shared his bowls of wine half and half with the thirsty Šarac. The spirit of these early epics, immortalized by oral tradition, was carried into our era by Pavle Dokić, the little-known last *hajduk* of Serbia.

Hajduks were a species of Robin Hood, brigands who lived in the forests. Their lives were passed in fighting all authorities, not just Turkish but, as time passed, servants of the Slavic rulers who sought to collect taxes or administer to restless subjects. Pavle was hiding from the gendarmes one day when he fell enamored of a beautiful shepherdess and raped her. The girl, also a fierce Serb, grabbed his knife and stabbed him in his privates as she died. Dokic, before he shot himself to avoid capture, wrote in a little diary found beside his corpse by a gendarme: "I will have a step like a wolf and I will travel like a hero and will feed like a wolf. I will be like God in heaven for now we have remained, only us two, He in heaven and I on earth. As we hajduks say, so it must be and there will always be us hajduks, for the forests without hajduks cannot be; as heaven without God."

That was in 1938. There have been no practicing hajduks since.

Belgrade, before its destruction in 1941, was a simple Balkan city typical of its inhabitants. The Serbs, who lived there, were largely classless, close to the land and different only in relative wealth and education. Indeed, the royal dynasty was descended from a rich, 19th century pig farmer.

I loved and admired the flamboyant South Slavs despite (or because of) their many faults and I have sought to demonstrate why by surviving into the 20th century as such a unique people, it was historically inevitable that they should produce unique leaders in time of chaos and confusion.

One such was Tito, not a Serb but a cousinly Croat. The Croatian heritage, like that of Serbians, was to rebel in search of national freedom. It was historical justice that Josip Broz, a Croat peasant who was drafted into Austro-Hungary's imperial army in 1914 and fought under the heights of Belgrade against the Serbs, should have returned almost forty years later as Marshal Tito to rule his countrymen, at last liberated from all Teutonic governance.

It was also inevitable that Milovan Djilas, the Montenegrin peasant boy who had joined Tito's Communist partisans, should have ultimately backed Tito in fighting off Russian claims to domination and then should have split with Tito on the very issue that freedom, even freedom to criticize, no matter how described, cannot be rationed. Both men were unique and therefore somewhat typical of the dauntless Yugoslavs. Both, being South Slavs, were bound to rebel against repression. And Djilas was as much fated to rise against Titoism, with its restrictions and its corruption, as each had been fated to rise against foreign embrace, whether from Nazi Germany or Soviet Russia.

The logic of Djilas' life has been that if one is born with a sprout of liberty in his soul, one must follow it to the logical end, no matter how difficult. Neither Tito, who led the most renowned guerrilla resistance of the Second World War, nor Djilas, who followed him blindly, had any other inspirational goal than freedom as each imagined it. Until a quarrel broke out between them, each conceived of that freedom in terms of Stalinist Communism and the goals outlined by the Kremlin after the Allied Victory of 1945. It was only when Djilas perceived that such victory was illusive and incomplete that he broke away, first from Stalin, then Tito.

These three men of differing ages, differing heritage, and differing character each represented a special and significant form of revolution. While Djilas was still a tad romping in Montenegro, Tito, as the young Josip Broz, worked for the Daimler Benz factory in Austria and occasionally acted as a racing driver for its cars. And Stalin, under various revolutionary noms de guerre, had left the religious seminary in Georgia, where he completed his formal education, and was robbing banks and engaging in violent terrorism to further the revolutionary cause of the emigré Communist, V. I. Lenin.

Despite the vicious brutality of his character, Stalin was undoubtedly the greatest of the trio. He left as his testament a Bolshevised Soviet Union that he had hoisted from early uncertainties to the status of global superpower. Tito rebelled against Stalinism and bequeathed to his own Yugoslav kinsmen and to the international revolutionary movement the concept of national communism. This, in turn, led to the accepted belief that each land was entitled to make its revolution in accord with its national circumstances and traditions. And Djilas, finally, rebelled against Titoism and sowed in sullen eastern Europe the belief that freedom from both dictatorship and corruption was the right of all people.

It is interesting that these three revolutionists should all have known each other, at one time converging in a single Communist movement wholly dominated by Stalin and then should have fallen out, ultimately representing highly different ideological doctrines. Stalin was the superpower nationalist. He sought successfully to build a vast, well-equipped army, a huge new fleet and air force, and an industrial technological infrastructure that enabled the Soviet Union to look down on all foreign nations but one, the United States. Tito, at first Stalin's ablest lieutenant in spreading Soviet influence and dogma throughout eastern Europe, ended up as the symbol of national Marxism. This latter then adjusted to the circumstances of each society where it spread and flowered as Eurocommunism. Djilas broke first with Stalin, when he supported Tito's valiant uprising against the great Soviet despot, and then acted against his personal idol, Tito, in a protest against despotism and corruption.

During World War II, the relationships between Tito and Djilas were warm and almost familial. Only after the postwar break between the two did personal dislike intrude. The corruption and personal aggrandizement of all the top leadership, most of all by Tito himself, met with Milovan's sharp, undisguised disdain. He was often criticized for this puritan streak by both the Politburo members and their wives, who glorified in their new and unaccustomed splendor.

Tito resented Djilas' undisguised failure to join the circle of adulatory admirers with which the new dictator preferred to surround himself. Like Napoleon I, he enjoyed being admired by his staff, both in private and in public, although it is impossible to measure the genuine affection with which Tito was regarded by his intimates.

Reflecting on his own development from ardent Stalinist to complete non-Communist, Djilas looks back to his student days and says: "There were two constants in our ideological education: the acceptance of the revolutionary Leninist side of Marxism and loyalty to the Soviet Union, which subsequently triumphed in the ideological acceptance of Stalin's theories." When Djilas started to have doubts about Stalin as an individual it meant that he was even having deeper doubts about Marxism. But the break with Stalin had to be followed by the break with Tito before these personal symbols wilted and turned him against Marxist ideology itself.

In a way one might explain the contrast between the revolutionary credos evolved by these three men as a series of political overhauls in three separate generations. Stalin, the eldest, moulded the Leninist pattern with which he was originally associated into a purely Russian pattern of monolithic dictatorship from the top. It was similar to but more effective than that of the Czarist regimes that preceded it. Tito's governance was not wholly different but less brutal. It was less autocratic because the people he ruled were not used to the absolute, Czarist form of despotism imitated so successfully by Stalin. And Djilasism, although it has not succeeded in replacing Titoism among the South Slav peoples, clearly had a relatively liberalizing effect on the expectations and also the governing methods that have prevailed in Yugoslavia since Tito's death.

One might say of Yugoslavia that the southern Slavs have become a kind of revolutionary cooking pot during the middle of the 20th century and ever since. Much as these three constrasting prophets of Marxism differed among themselves, all three were of modest parentage, all three were born in monarchic states—the Imperial Czarist empire, the Austro-Hungarian empire, and the tiny kingdom of Montenegro—and the first two were surely corrupted by power. Djilas, who never held the reins of autocracy, could not have been tainted by it. His tastes and character are too pure in their simplicity.

Stalinism, an evil absolutism, fell prey to Titoism in its Western imperial domains from Poland to Yugoslavia. Titoism, in its uncertain experiments with democratic procedures, ruled out Stalinism as the answer. Djilasism is almost certainly a premature formula for

experimentation in East Europe. It is probably the name of the political game to be played out there. That area has already given
signs of subconscious belief in Alexis de Toqueville's formulation:
"Despotism . . . which is at all times dangerous, is most particularly to be feared in democratic ages." Djilas himself wrote:

Our country will not be bureaucratic and Stalinist even if it wants to and
cannot even if it should be. Stalin was unique. His epoch is passing, and
with it Stalinism. He rose to the top when the bureaucracy was rising.
But today, the apex of bureaucratic Communism has already been attained
and now the bureaucracy is in its decline. Its future may hold pain, tragedy and cruelty, but not victory.

Our Yugoslav Stalinism [Titoism] in part inherited but in greater measure developed on our own soil, can now only make retreats—longer or
shorter, more or less painful. Stalinism in Yugoslavia is and will remain
something alien, something imposed, which will never bring victory and
glory to our country. It is not suited to us because we are already part of
democratic and humanistic mankind; or if we are not yet, we will be, we
must be to live and to survive.[1]

Although it soon became plain that Tito, in facing down Stalin
and promoting national modification of Leninist theorems, had
charted a new course for European Communists, he never made
any boastful claims in this respect. As early as May 16, 1968, Tito
told me: "People in other countries are trying to democratize and
liberalize situations that had previously been stagnant. It doesn't mean
they will follow the same path we have pursued in Yugoslavia. But
practice in the past has shown that changes are necessary. We are
dialecticians and we know that what is good today, or necessary
today, becomes neither as good nor as necessary tomorrow. . . .
Marxism must be applied according to conditions prevailing in any
country; and these differ everywhere."[2]

Tito did not claim to be a prophet, a teacher; only a discoverer,
an analyst. He never referred to a "Titoist" movement and he never
laid claim to any parenthood of what came to be known as "Eurocommunism." Not by nature a modest man, Tito showed in this
that he was not vainglorious either.

And, unlike other 20th century revolutionists, given to bombast,
Djilas is content with anonymity for his own ideas and an entire
absence of power himself for, as he says, "There is nothing wrong

with being an ordinary person who loves his little pleasures and who lives from them. That is what life is all about . . . ."³

Milovan's contribution to political theory, a modified Acton's Law, was that Communism as a system is installed by force and, when established in authority, retains absolute authority, brooking no opposition. (The Vladivostok elections in Russia, held in 1917, represent the only free vote ever staged in the Marxist realm where an honest majority was won by the Communists. None other; anywhere!)

THE YUGOSLAV HEDGEHOG'S ONE BIG LESSON

Lord Acton postulated: power corrupts; absolute power corrupts absolutely.

As earlier recalled, Professor Isaiah Berlin wrote that the fox knows many things but the hedgehog knows one big thing. The one big thing Djilas has contributed is the elaboration to Marxism of Lord Acton's law.

In a Marxist-Leninist state all power is in the hands of the omnipowerful state bureaucracy. Therefore this bureaucracy is predestined to absolute corruption.

Because it runs and administers everything, such a country is governed by a totally corrupt administration at all levels. No such system can survive indefinitely. Djilas perceived that since the state becomes owner of most industrial and agricultural enterprises, it establishes a vast bureaucracy wherever it gains control. This bureaucracy inevitably becomes corrupt since its sponsors are human beings and greedy.

To Milovan's horror he saw the Soviet theorem largely mirrored in his own Yugoslavia. His protests against corrupted power in authority inevitably led to a quarrel with the symbol of absolute power, Tito. And ultimately, on reflection it was applied in his mind to all uniparty Marxist states of the contemporary world.

Analysing his own ideological development, Djilas now says:

Power engenders suspicion in a man's psychology. He becomes unable to live without power. It corrupts him. In the end it didn't succeed in corrupting me; but it corrupts. . . . I began my new life as an author. I started out as a writer and only later became a revolutionary. Now I am again a writer.

Today I do not really know if I am in *any* way a Marxist. I'm surely a democratic socialist—not a regular Social-Democrat in the Western sense. I'm an atheist. I'm a materialist. But not in a Marxist sense. Marxism is outdated. It is old-fashioned. The human being and modern society are too complex to be adjusted to Hegelian dialectics.

I am not a religious man but I know that a human being must have conscience and morality. I agree with what religion teaches: that a man must believe in something. But not in God.

All versions of Communism are becoming decadent. They must inevitably change into a democratic society. Communism is a combustive warrior's concept and organization. Society cannot bear to exist indefinitely within such a tense atmosphere.[4]

In this era of "isms," when millions of people have been condemned by history to sacrifice what liberty they knew or had dreamed of to totemic structure of the state, it is noteworthy that a man who had been a prisoner of this type of system, then of its successor, a relatively more liberal modification, was sufficiently strong-willed and imaginative enough to envision further and logical goals. For the better part of thirty years he strove to achieve these aims. His life is a testimonial to human determination and capacity to bear suffering with no other quest than freedom.

Philosophically Djilas reckons that he is a "free" man. For years he could not travel abroad or publish his writings in his native land. But he can now do both. He can travel to wherever he wishes, and this means a great deal to him because it permits him to visit his son, in England and America.

Now Milovan is no longer in jail or even under house arrest, and no longer confined to Yugoslavia. He considers himself a free man because there is no longer a proscription on his writings, because he can travel abroad, because he is no longer in prison, and, above all, because he is no longer regarded as an official enemy. Freedom cannot be rationed; now he *feels* free and is therefore happy at the end of an arduous life in a hostile world. He yielded no concession to regain Paradise.

NOTES

1. *Parts of a Lifetime.* Op. cit., p. 244.
2. Conversation with the Author.
3. Ibid.
4. Ibid.

Bibliography

Clissold, Stephen. *Djilas, the Progress of a Revolutionary*. Middlesex: Maurice Temple Smith, 1983.

Deakin, F. W. D. *The Embattled Mountain*. London: Oxford University Press, 1971.

Djilas, Milovan. *The New Class—An Analysis of the Communist System*. New York: Frederick A. Praeger, 1957.

Djilas, Milovan. *Conversations with Stalin*. New York: Harcourt, Brace & World, 1962.

Djilas, Milovan. *Montenegro*. New York: Harcourt, Brace and World, 1962.

Djilas, Milovan. *The Leper and Other Stories*. New York: Harcourt, Brace and World, 1964.

Djilas, Milovan. *The Unperfect Society—Beyond the New Class*. London: Methuen and Co., 1969.

Djilas, Milovan. *The Stone and the Violets*. New York: Harcourt, Brace, Jovanovich, 1971.

Djilas, Milovan. *Wartime—With Tito and the Partisans*. London: Martin Secker and Warburg, 1977.

Djilas, Milovan. *Rise and Fall*. New York: Harcourt, Brace, Jovanovich, 1985.

Maclean, Fitzroy. *Disputed Barricade*. London: Jonathan Cape, 1957.

Milenkovitch, M. and D. (Eds.). *Parts of a Lifetime*. New York: Harcourt, Brace, Jovanovich, 1980.

Njegos, Prince Petar Petrovic. *The Mountain Wreath*. Translated by James W. Wiles. London: George Allen and Unwin Ltd., 1939.

Sulzberger, C. L. *A Long Row of Candles*. New York: Macmillan, 1969.

Sulzberger, C. L. *The Last of the Giants*. New York: Macmillan, 1970.

Sulzberger, C. L. *An Age of Mediocrity*. New York: Macmillan, 1973.

Sulzberger, C. L. *Postscript with a Chinese Accent*. New York: Macmillan, 1974.

Index

About the Author

C. L. SULZBERGER, former head of the Foreign Service (Worldwide) of the *New York Times* and author of the column, "Foreign Affairs," is the author of twenty-four books, including biographies, memoirs, histories, and novels. Before joining the *Times* in 1939, he worked for the *Pittsburgh Press, United Press, North American Newspaper Alliance,* and *London Evening Standard.* He has visited and written from all corners of the globe including all seven continents, and among the awards he has received are several Overseas Press Club prizes and a Pulitzer citation. Retired from journalism since 1977, he currently resides in Paris.